JAPANESE QUILT

INSPIRATIONS Susan Briscoe

JAPANESE QUILT
INSPIRATIONS
Susan
Briscoe

14 easy-to-make projects using Japanese fabrics

David and Charles

www.rucraft.co.uk

For all my quilting friends, worldwide.

A DAVID & CHARLES BOOK
Copyright © David & Charles Limited 2011

David & Charles is an F+W Media Inc. company
4700 East Galbraith Road, Cincinnati, OH 45236

First published in the UK and US in 2011

Text and designs copyright © Susan Briscoe 2011
Layout and photography copyright © David & Charles 2011

All photography shot at The Japanese Garden & Bonsai Nursery
(www.thebonsainursery.com)

A catalogue record for this book is available from the
British Library.

ISBN-13: 978-0-7153-3827-8 paperback
ISBN-10: 0-7153-3827-7 paperback

Printed in China by RR Donnelley
for David & Charles
Brunel House   Newton Abbot   Devon

Publisher Alison Myer
Commissioning Editor Cheryl Brown
Editor James Brooks
Project Editor Lin Clements
Designer Victoria Marks
Photographers Lorna Yabsley and Karl Adamson
Production Controller Kelly Smith
Pre Press Natasha Jorden

David & Charles publish high quality books on a wide range of subjects.
For more great book ideas visit: www.rucraft.co.uk

Contents

Introduction

Japanese fabrics appeal to quilters worldwide, who often seek a special quilt project to feature these gorgeous materials to their best advantage. Inspired by the imagery I found all around me when I lived in Japan, here are ten quilts and four smaller projects reflecting traditional Japanese patterns and motifs which will feature your Japanese fabrics in an authentic style. Designed to let the fabrics take centre stage, they use the easiest methods to obtain the maximum effect.

When I went to work in the north of Japan, in a small town called Yuza-machi in Yamagata Prefecture, I was inspired to begin quilting by the geometric designs I saw in traditional architecture, design and crafts. The subtle shades of the landscape, the unusual colour combinations in kimono ensembles, the tea ceremony and local festivals – all were a treasure trove of ideas. Yamagata Prefecture is noted in Japan for its festivals and culture, shaped by its historical importance in trades such as *benibana* (safflower) cultivation and rice production. By chance I was in the ideal place to absorb some of the diverse visual language of this fascinating country. My experiences there continue to influence my quilts.

The quilts and projects I have created for you explore many fabric themes, from the blues and browns essential for Japanese country style to richly coloured gold prints and kimono silks evocative of sumptuous treasures. There are quilts for large scale feature panels (Furoshiki and Hanui), and quilts that use narrow strips in easy ways (Sakiori, Masu and Sensu). Landscape prints can come into their own as block centres (Kunimoto) and stripes and directional fabrics give movement to blocks (Irori). The shape of the kimono itself is an unusual appliqué outline to display gold prints (Kimono). Multicoloured scraps (Shimacho) or a two-colour theme (Igeta) offer more ideas. Blocks from the quilts are used in different ways to make four smaller projects, which can be treated as block tasters or as ways to use up spare patchwork from the quilts.

In addition to ideas for working with traditional Japanese fabrics, such as cotton yukata and silk kimono cloth, the patchwork explores the use of Japanese-themed strip cuts, fat quarters and other specially created collections, including large, printed feature panels. The quilts are not dependent on having exactly the same prints and six designs are presented twice in different fabric themes, suggesting other creative and quilting options. There are instructions for the easy patchwork and appliqué methods used. Ideas for hand and machine quilting are provided, including sashiko-style 'big stitch' quilting. Ten of the quilts showcase professional machine quilting on long-arm machines – see Suppliers for details – offering the ideal finishing solution if you don't want to quilt a large piece yourself.

It all starts with the fabrics…

Fabrics

Japanese fabrics, made in Japan, and Japanese style fabrics, produced outside of Japan, can be combined successfully to make beautiful, unique quilts. Whether your taste is for the bright hues of children's kimono, the shades of Japanese maples in autumn, the fresh blue and white of cotton yukata kimono or the blues and browns of country fabrics, you can use these in your quilts. A selection of fabric suppliers is listed in Suppliers.

Old and New Fabrics

Because 100% cotton can be pressed to give a crisp seam, it is the easiest to use for patchwork and appliqué. Many traditional Japanese fabrics are reproduced as cotton prints, some with dobby or sateen weaves for textural interest. Patterns range from tiny designs to large-scale patterns, which can be used together and are frequently produced as a complete collection for patchwork, like the majority of the fabrics used for the Irori Quilt. Fabrics can easily be mixed and matched from many manufacturers and across different ranges, such as the scrap strips used for the alternate version of the Sakiori Quilt. American cotton stripes and checks blend in well for the Japanese country look, although the dark blue may be more ultramarine than indigo. Faux patchwork fabrics reflect the Japanese traditions of *boromono* (rag cloth patchwork) and, on a more sophisticated level, *shikishi* (poem card motifs) are often shown overlapped.

Traditional Japanese fabrics for kimono are narrow width, approximately 14¼in (36.2cm). These may be silk, cotton, wool or various blends. Cotton fabrics with woven patterns suitable for patchwork include *shima* (stripes), *koshi* (checks), *kasuri* (ikat) and *tsumugi* (a slubbed weave). Fabrics salvaged from damaged kimono are often used for patchwork by Japanese quilters, but think twice before cutting up an old kimono for patchwork yourself – you may have an interesting antique, and vintage kimono are a finite source of patchwork material. Old fabrics may also be weak. Soft, recycled kimono silks, like *chirimen* (crêpe) can be backed with a lightweight iron-on interfacing for patchwork. Cottons are easier to sew but silk can add a special glow to a quilt, like the autumnal tones used for Kunimoto Quilt. *Tsumugi* is woven in silk as well as cotton and was used for the chequerboard blocks in the same quilt.

Japanese-style patchwork prints, reproduction traditional fabrics and kimono silks include different textures, from glossy to homespun weaves.

Furoshiki (wrapping cloth) are intended for wrapping goods and gifts but their bold pictorial designs make great quilt panels — see the Furoshiki Quilt. Similar large designs are printed as quilt panels, as shown here.

Dyed patterns include large and small motifs. Freehand *yuzen* rice paste-resist dyeing, invented around 1700, is used for formal silk kimono, sometimes with silk or gold embroidery. These designs are frequently reproduced in quilting fabrics, with the gold accents added in a metallic print, such as the floral designs used for Kimono Quilt. *Komon* (small patterns) are smaller designs, with tiny *edo komon* patterns stencilled in just two colours, similar to tone-on-tone patchwork fabric.

Katazome, large-scale stencilled fabric, usually indigo and white, used to be made for household textiles, such as futon covers, and is now reproduced for quilting. Patchwork prints of *shibori* (tie dye) and *kasuri* (ikat) recreate affordable copies of expensive fabrics. Contemporary stencil-dyed cottons, like *yukata* fabrics for summer casual kimono, usually have large patterns, ideal for featuring in the fan appliqués in the Sensu Quilt, where the background is a *shibori* print. Men's and boy's *yukata* favour smaller geometric patterns, such as the *igeta* motifs used for the kimono appliqué backgrounds on the Ranna Table Runner.

Trusted Tip…

Generous fabric quantities are given in the You Will Need list for each project, but if you wish to select a particular motif ('fussy cutting') or want to use a directional fabric in your quilt, it is advisable to add a little more.

Gold metallic prints in rich colours, bright contemporary yukata cottons and traditional indigo fabrics can be combined in your quilts for unique results.

Vintage kimono silks from the 1970s and 1980s, fresh from the bolt, were used for the Kunimoto Quilt.

Fabric Sizes

Quilt shops usually sell fabric in smaller pieces as well as by the whole and half yard (metre). Patchwork fabrics are usually 42in–44in (106.7cm–111.8cm) wide. Fat quarters and fat eighths are often sold in coordinated packs, sometimes including a whole fabric range. A fat quarter pack was used to make the Irori Quilt, with some extra fabrics added. Common pre-cut sizes are as follows:

- Fat quarter – a yard (or metre) quartered by cutting vertically as well as horizontally to make squarish pieces about 18in x 21in–22in (45.7cm x 53.3cm–55.9cm).
- Thin quarter – a yard (or metre) cut into four strips widthways.
- Fat eighth – a fat quarter cut in half.
- 10in (25.4cm) squares.

Packs of strips are also popular. Some are packaged by fabric manufacturers, others cut and packed by the shop. Strip cuts were used to make both versions of the Masu Quilt and the Sakiori Quilt. Manufacturers' strip cuts usually include a full coordinated range of fabrics; shops may include fabrics from different but complementary fabric collections. They may be sold as a roll or packaged as a block. Different manufacturers have different names for these cuts but the basic sizes are as follows:

- Strips 2½in (6.4cm) wide – cut across the fabric width, making strips 2½in x 42in–44in (6.4cm x 106.7cm–111.8cm).
- Strips 1½in (3.8cm) wide – cut across the fabric width, making strips 1½in x 42in–44in (3.8cm x 106.7cm–111.8cm).

Pre-cut strip rolls and 10in (25.4cm) squares include a variety of prints and are a convenient way to buy fabric.

Japanese kimono fabrics are approximately 14¼in (36.2cm) wide. Kimono shops in Japan sell complete rolls only, with 13 yards (12 metres) approximately on one roll to make one kimono. Shops selling kimono fabric for patchwork will either sell by the yard (metre) from the bolt or pieces recycled from used kimono. Recycled pieces will include half-width pieces used for the kimono front overlap panels and collar sections. Because the kimono has no shoulder seam, fabric recycled from the main body panels will have a slit cut for the neck at around 55in–60in (139.7cm–152.4cm) from one end. Sleeve pieces will measure approximately 40in x 14¼in (101.6cm x 36.5cm). It may, therefore, be necessary to piece recycled fabrics to use for larger quilt sections, like borders.

Measurements

The projects in this book were made using imperial inches. Metric conversions are given in brackets but use *either* imperial *or* metric, as the systems are not strictly interchangeable. The best results will be obtained using inches.

Japanese Motifs and Their Meanings

Some Japanese floral motifs are very familiar but flowers and leaves should ideally be used slightly in advance of their season if you want to give your project a seasonal theme. Twelve different flowers and leaves are used for the Kimono Quilt, with one kimono block representing each month of the year. Stylized flowers and leaves can be used at any time, as can *kisho-mon* (auspicious patterns), and multiple season flowers in one pattern can be used all year long. Flowers, leaves and animals frequently used as fabric motifs include the following.

Spring
- *ume* – plum blossom
- *sakura* – cherry blossom
- *tsutsuji* – azalea
- *fuji* – wisteria
- *chōcho* – butterfly

Summer
- *botan* – peony
- *tachibana* – mandarin orange blossom
- *kiri* – paulownia
- *ayame* – iris
- *himawari* – sunflower
- *nadeshiko* – carnation
- *yuri* – lily

Autumn
- *momiji* – red maple leaves
- *kaki* – persimmon fruit
- *tsuta* – ivy
- *asagao* – morning glory
- *kiku* – chrysanthemum
- *hagi* – bush clover

- *kikyō* – bellflower
- *kusa no hana* – autumn grasses and flowers
- *tsuki* – moon
- *tonbo* – dragonfly

Winter
- *kantsubaki* – winter camellia
- *nanten no mi* – nandina berries
- *taka* – hawk
- *chidori* – plovers
See also *shō chiku bai* below

Auspicious Patterns
Kisho-mon include:
- *shō chiku bai* – pine, plum and bamboo – the 'three friends of winter'
- *matsu* (pine) – long life, the home of the gods
- *take* (bamboo) – endurance
- *tsuru* (crane) – long life
- *tsuru kame* (crane and tortoise) – long life

- *kikkō* (tortoiseshell hexagon) – long life
- *hōō* (phoenix) – peace and prosperity
- *ōgi* (folding fan) – increase
- *noshi* (bundle of dried abalone strips) – increase
- *koi* (carp) – advancement in life
- *ryu* (dragon) – leadership

Collection of Treasures
Takara-zukushi include:
- *hōjyu* – wish-granting jewel
- *kakure gasa* – straw hat of invisibility
- *kakure mino* – straw cloak of invisibility
- *kinchaku* – treasure bag
- *hōyaku* – treasure house key
- *gunbai* – referee's fan
- *uchideno-kozuchi* – wish-granting mallet

The Quilts

This section has sixteen gorgeous quilts you can make using ten patterns from traditional Japanese sources. Each quilt starts with a collection of Japanese fabrics and my inspiration for the quilt is shown in snapshots, with suggestions on fabrics you might use. There is a varied range of patchwork techniques to explore, producing some fascinating effects. Many of the quilts have been created in two different colourways, showing how different a design can look. Different quilting designs, either hand quilted or long-arm machine quilted, add variety to the finished quilts.

Furoshiki
Wrapping Cloth

Decorative wrapping cloths known as *furoshiki* are popular souvenirs from Japan and a great present for a quilter, and they are sold in most souvenir shops. This subtly coloured design of *akikusa* (autumn grasses), with cute leaping rabbits, immediately suggested a quilt centre. A simple strip border frames the design in similar colours to the centre panel. The strips are assembled using Seminole patchwork, sewing the opposite border strips at the same time, so the strips are arranged in the same sequence. A plain rust border brings extra colour while retaining the mainly indigo country style. The quilt was free-motion long-arm quilted in a variety of patterns inspired by the fabric prints and traditional Japanese designs.

Furoshiki are still used every day in Japan and also as a traditional gift wrap — the recipient is supposed to return it with another gift inside. They are popular souvenirs in Asakusa, Tokyo, where gift shops line the avenue up to the Sensoji temple.

Fabric Focus

Furoshiki are made in silk and rayon as well as cotton, but for a washable quilt cotton is best. They are squarish rectangles, typically 1in (2.5cm) or so longer than wide. The selvedges are usually left on, so you will just need to trim off the hem at the top and bottom. Several quilt fabric manufacturers specialize in Japanese style panels which make an excellent *furoshiki* substitute, or you can simply use any large scale Japanese print that is too lovely to cut up.

Furoshiki Quilt

You will need

- One *furoshiki* or similar panel, 44½in x 45½in (113cm x 115.6cm) – others sizes may be used, see step 1

- Fifteen to eighteen fat quarters, for cutting 1½in x 22in (3.8cm x 55.9cm) strips

- For russet inner and outer borders (matching) 70in x 12½in (177.8cm x 31.7cm) (see step 7 and tip below):
  two strips 44½in x 1½in (113cm x 3.8cm)
  two strips 47½in x 1½in (120.7cm x 3.8cm)
  two strips 66½in x 1½in (168.9cm x (3.8cm)
  two strips 69½in x 1½in (176.5cm x 3.8cm)

- Sewing thread to tone with patchwork

- Quilting thread to contrast with patchwork (if machine quilting)

- Backing fabric to coordinate with patchwork – see Wadding and Backing

- Wadding (batting) – see Wadding and Backing

- Binding fabric 300in (762cm) length

Finished quilt: 69in x 68½in (175.3cm x 174cm) approximately

Trusted Tip...

The patchwork border strips can be cut from more fat quarters if you wish, from scrap pieces or 1½in (3.8cm) wide strip cuts, providing they are long enough to cut two 10½in (26.7cm) long sections from each strip (excluding selvedge). If the majority of strips include the *furoshiki* or panel colours, the border will coordinate just fine. The exact number of strips required will depend on your centre panel size – see step 1.

Measuring the Centre Panel

1 Before starting to make the border strips, measure the size of your centre panel to work out how many strips you need to cut. The *furoshiki* used here was slightly larger than 44½in x 45½in (113cm x 115.6cm). Make a note of the measurements but do not cut the panel down to size just yet. Add on 2in (5cm) to both of your measurements to allow for the inner border and use these numbers to work out how many border strips you will need, i.e., forty-seven strips for each side and forty-six strips for the top and bottom borders. With so many seams between the border strips, it is likely that the finished borders will measure slightly shorter than expected, and it is easier to simply adjust the centre panel and inner border to fit the patchwork borders rather than vice versa (described in steps 6 and 7). A further twenty strips will be needed for the border corners. The exact size of inner and outer borders, number of border patchwork strips and size of the finished quilt will depend on the size of your centre panel.

Cutting the Fabric

2 Following step 1, for this *furoshiki* with the inner border added (finished width 1in/2.5cm), forty-six 1½in (3.8cm) strips are required across the top and bottom of the quilt, with sixty-seven in total up each side (which includes the ten strips for each corner). Each strip you cut from the fat quarter will make two border patchwork strips. To make the quilt as shown, cut 113 strips 1½in (3.8cm) wide, across the width of the fat quarters, so the strips will measure between 21½in (54.6cm) and 22in (55.9cm) long, as the border will be 10½in (26.7cm) wide. Leave the selvedges on for the moment.

Sewing the Patchwork

3 Using ¼in (6mm) seams throughout, machine sew pairs of strips together, starting at the opposite end from the selvedge. Continue sewing the strips into six groups of eight strips for the sides, plus one group of nine and another of ten (sixty-seven strips in total), leaving the group of ten separate for now. Sew five groups of eight to make the top and bottom borders, plus one group of six (forty-six strips in total). These are manageable sizes for cutting in step 4 but sewing the total length of each border together at this stage would make the next cut difficult to do. Press each piece of patchwork so all the seams lie in the same direction.

4 From each set of strips, cut two 10½in (26.7cm) wide sections of patchwork, lining up with the opposite end from the selvedges for your first cut, as shown by the red lines in Fig 1. Each set of strips will make two identical patchwork sections for the border. Use the same strips on either side or top and bottom of the quilt, so the repetition of colours and patterns gives a subtle rhythm to the borders, rather than a totally random scrap look.

5 Machine sew the patchwork sections together to make the border strips, as in Fig 2. Press all seams in the same direction. Turn the two 10½in x 10½in (26.7cm x 26.7cm) sections through 90 degrees so the strips run at right angles to the main border strips, and then sew to the bottom of the left border and the top of the right border, creating the effect of continually overlapping borders aound the quilt, completing the borders.

Adding the Borders

6 Measure the length of the top and bottom patchwork borders and note the measurements. Subtract 2in (5cm) to get the width for the centre panel – e.g., 44½in (113cm). Measure the length of the side border, excluding the ten strips at each end, add ½in (1.3cm) to replace the seam allowance lost in the patchwork and subtract 2in (5cm) from this total to get the length for the centre panel. Trim the centre panel to match these measurements.

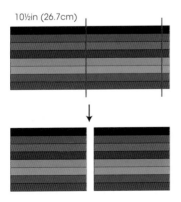

10½in (26.7cm)

Fig 1

Fig 2

7 Cut the inner narrow border pieces to length from the 70in x 12½in (177.8cm x 31.7cm) piece. The top and bottom border length should be the same measurement as the width of the panel, i.e., 44½in (113cm) for the quilt shown here. The side border strip should measure the length of the panel plus 2in (5cm), to allow for the width of the top and bottom borders, i.e., 47½in x 1½in (120.7cm x 3.8cm) for the quilt shown here. Machine sew the top and bottom narrow borders to the quilt top and press towards the outside of the quilt. Machine sew the side narrow borders to the centre panel. Press towards the outside again.

8 Machine sew the top and bottom patchwork border to the quilt. A few patchwork border seam allowances lie in the same direction as those in the previous border, so just flip them the opposite way as you sew, so the seams lie snugly together. Press towards the quilt centre. Machine sew the side patchwork borders in the same way. Measure and trim the top and bottom narrow outer border to match the width of the quilt and sew to the top and bottom, pressing towards the outside, i.e., 66½in x 1½in (168.9cm x 3.8cm) for the quilt shown here. Measure and trim the side narrow borders to match the length of the quilt and sew to the sides, pressing towards the outside to finish the quilt top, i.e., 69½in x 1½in (176.5cm x 3.8cm) for the quilt shown here.

Quilting and Finishing

9 Layer and tack (baste) the quilt ready for quilting, if quilting by hand or domestic machine – see Making a Quilt Sandwich. The blue and brown quilt was long-arm machine quilted, with the machine guided by hand in various free-hand designs suggested by the fabric patterns and the freely drawn designs of *tsutsugaki* (freehand paste-resist dyeing). Continuous lines like these can be free-motion quilted on domestic machines although the long-arm machine operator can 'draw' larger gentle curves in a more flowing style than is easily achieved on a conventional sewing machine.

Trusted Tip...

Any quilt that has a picture panel as the main focus needs to be quilted with sensitivity to the overall design of the image. Use lines and motifs in the panel as the starting point rather than imposing an unrelated pattern all over the panel.

10 Bind your quilt to finish – see Binding. Select a binding fabric to coordinate with your quilt, such as the dark blue used here, which contrasts with the outer border fabric.

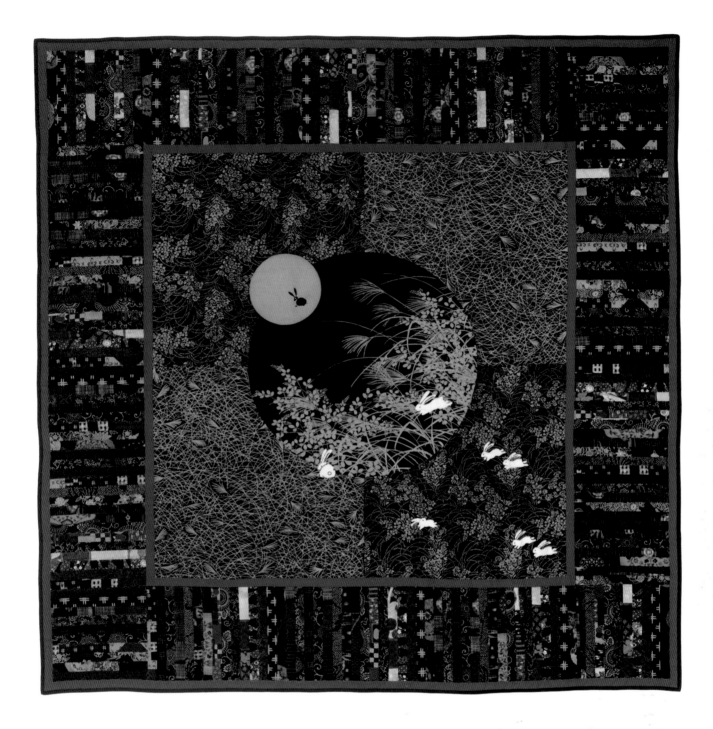

The rabbit and moon panel makes a charming centre for this quilt. According to Japanese folklore, the moon shows a pair of rabbits making rice cakes, hence the moon's association with rabbits. The repetitive sequence of the opposite borders in this quilt is subtle but helps to give a sense of order to the patchwork strips. Inspired by the fabric prints and traditional Japanese designs, a variety of patterns were free-motion long-arm quilted. The brighter panel shown overleaf also influences the quilting, with the main motifs outlined and the border strips hand quilted in the ditch.

Long-arm quilter: Ferret (see Suppliers)

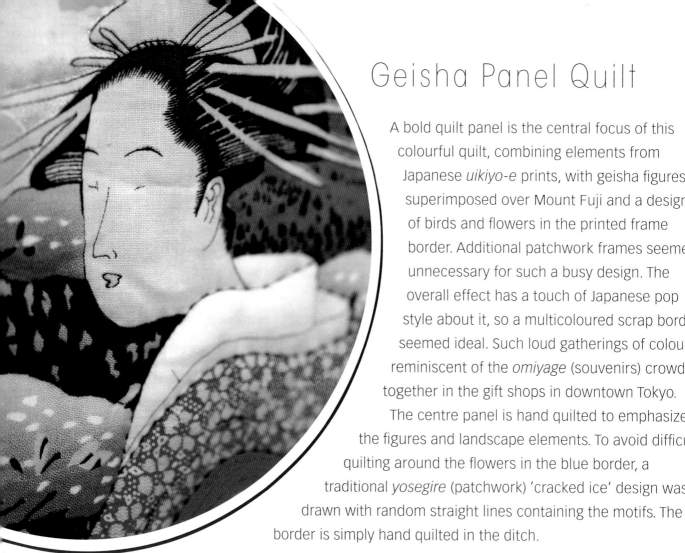

Geisha Panel Quilt

A bold quilt panel is the central focus of this colourful quilt, combining elements from Japanese *uikiyo-e* prints, with geisha figures superimposed over Mount Fuji and a design of birds and flowers in the printed frame border. Additional patchwork frames seemed unnecessary for such a busy design. The overall effect has a touch of Japanese pop style about it, so a multicoloured scrap border seemed ideal. Such loud gatherings of colour are reminiscent of the *omiyage* (souvenirs) crowded together in the gift shops in downtown Tokyo.

The centre panel is hand quilted to emphasize the figures and landscape elements. To avoid difficult quilting around the flowers in the blue border, a traditional *yosegire* (patchwork) 'cracked ice' design was drawn with random straight lines containing the motifs. The border is simply hand quilted in the ditch.

Paper lanterns and hanging ornaments in various traditional styles are packed together in gift shops on the Nakamise-dori in downtown Tokyo. A combination of clashing colours and shiny golden glitter is hard to resist!

Kunimoto

Hometown

Japanese architecture is a never-ending source of inspiration for patchwork designs and one of these quilt blocks was based on the circular windows in a modern pavilion constructed for traditional arts, including tea ceremony. Two different 10in (25.4cm) blocks are set out in a chequerboard to make the quilt centre. The landscape fabric circles are machine appliquéd and the borders are added using part-sewn seams. The circle block borders and chequerboards, quick to make using Seminole patchwork, are pieced with 2½in (6.4cm) wide strips. The fabrics used are kimono silks in glowing autumnal colours, enhanced with free-hand long-arm machine quilting. The design is also suitable for making in cottons and for hand quilting.

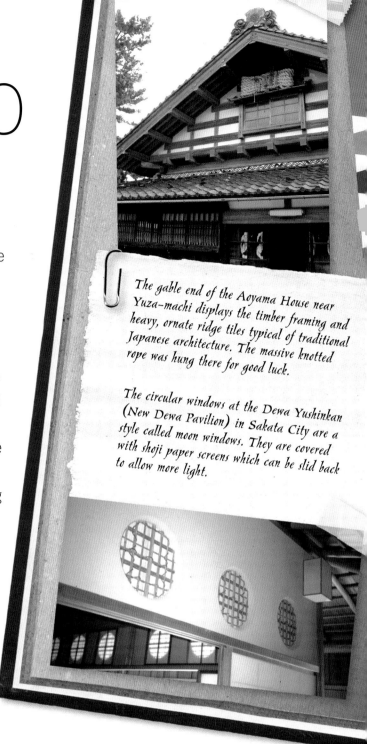

The gable end of the Aoyama House near Yuza-machi displays the timber framing and heavy, ornate ridge tiles typical of traditional Japanese architecture. The massive knotted rope was hung there for good luck.

The circular windows at the Dewa Yushinkan (New Dewa Pavilion) in Sakata City are a style called moon windows. They are covered with shoji paper screens which can be slid back to allow more light.

Fabric Focus

The circle appliqués are the perfect place to feature a landscape design. Freezer paper appliqué is a good technique for kimono silks, which can have a very soft drape and be difficult to handle without a support underneath. The quilt combines soft *rinzu* (silk damask) for the lemon squares and softer *chirimen* (crêpe) in the border with crisp *tsumugi* (spun) silk. Use iron-on interfacing if required to give soft silks more body before cutting out the patchwork pieces. A woven stripe is a good choice for the circle block borders.

Kunimoto Quilt

You will need

- For the circle blocks:
  ½yd (0.5m) landscape fabric or similar for circles
  ½yd (0.5m) of fabric for block centres
  27in x 43in–44in fabric (68.6cm x 109.2cm–112cm) for striped borders

- For the chequerboard blocks (see panel opposite):
  three strips 91in x 2½in (231.1cm x 6.4cm) rust
  two strips 91in x 2½in (231.1cm x 6.4cm) green
  three strips 61in x 2½in (155cm x 6.4cm) green
  two strips 61in x 2½in (155cm x 6.4cm) rust

- For the narrow border:
  two strips 50½in x 1½in (128.3cm x 3.8cm)
  two strips 52½in x 1½in (133.4cm x 3.8cm)

- Four strips 59in x 7in (149.9cm x 17.8cm)
  for border (about half the width of the
  kimono fabric)

- Thirteen 5in (12.7cm) diameter freezer
  paper circles

- Sewing thread to tone with patchwork (use silk
  for silk, if possible)

- Quilting thread to contrast with patchwork
  (if machine quilting)

- Backing fabric to coordinate with patchwork –
  see Wadding and Backing

- Wadding (batting) – see Wadding and Backing

- Binding fabric 280in (711.2cm) length

Finished quilt: 66in (167.6cm) square approximately

Trusted Tip...

A pack of forty 2½in (6.4cm) wide patchwork cotton strips could be used for the thirteen circle block borders, four 8½in (21.6cm) long each, and the twelve chequerboard blocks, which each need twenty-five 2½in (6.4cm) squares. These could be cut and arranged as individual squares rather than using the Seminole technique instructions in step 6, perhaps using similar fabrics to create an X-effect in each chequerboard.

Working with Kimono Fabric or Patchwork Fabric

The Kunimoto Quilt was made entirely from silk kimono fabrics which are only about 14¼in (36.2cm) wide. The yardage quantities opposite have been calculated to allow ample fabric from standard-width patchwork fabric as an alternative. If using standard-width fabric, you could work with shorter strips cut across the fabric width rather than very long strips as listed for the checkerboard blocks – two and a half strips cut across the width would substitute for each of the longer strips and one and a half strips for the shorter ones.

If using narrow 14¼in (36.2cm) wide kimono fabric, you will need 40in (101.6cm) for the circles and the background squares, with 94in (238.8cm) for the block borders. Five 2½in (6.4cm) wide strips can be cut across the kimono fabric width, so a 91in (231.1cm) length of each chequerboard fabric is required. The wide outer borders can be cut from 120in (305cm) and about half the width of the kimono fabric. The four narrow borders can be cut from one 53in x 6½in (134.6cm x 16.5cm) piece. Iron ultra lightweight iron-on interfacing to the back of each piece before cutting out if necessary, except the circles (see Fabric Focus at the start of this chapter).

All sizes above are generous to allow a little leeway in cutting. Patchwork cottons and kimono silks can be mixed if you wish. See Fabrics for more information.

Cutting the Fabric

1 Using the iron on a cool setting, iron the thirteen circles of freezer paper – see Equipment and Materials on to the back of the landscape feature fabric, arranging the circles so that attractive 'views' are obtained and with the circles no less than ¾in (1.9cm) apart. Cut out the circles, allowing a generous ¼in–⅜in (6mm–1cm) hem allowance all round, as in Fig 1.

2 Cut thirteen 6½in (16.5cm) squares for the circle block centres. Cut eleven 2½in (6.4cm) strips across the width of the border fabrics and cut fifty-two 8½in x 2½in (21.6cm x 6.4cm) pieces from these strips. If using kimono-width fabric, you will need to cut 8½in (21.6cm) wide strips *across* the fabric and cut each strip into five 8½in x 2½in (21.6cm x 6.4cm) pieces.

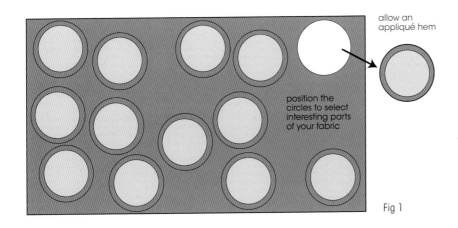

allow an appliqué hem

position the circles to select interesting parts of your fabric

Fig 1

Making the Appliqué

3 Press the hem allowance over the edge of the freezer paper circles with the iron on a slightly higher temperature, being careful not to scorch your fabrics and only pressing the very edge. Allow the pieces to cool. Pin one circle to the centre backing square, so the freezer paper is sandwiched between the appliqué circle and the backing square, with the raw edges all tucked under, arranging the pins as shown in Fig 2. You can check it is central by measuring the space between the edges of the circle and the sides of the square, which should be approximately ¾in (1.9cm).

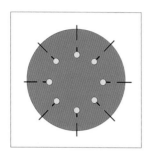

Fig 2

4 The appliqué can be hand or machine sewn to the backing square – see Appliqué. Once finished, cut a vertical slit behind the circle in the background fabric, taking care not to cut the circle itself, and remove the freezer paper by scrunching it up and pulling it out through the slit. Scrunching up the fabric a little around the circle edge helps to loosen the paper where it may have been caught by the appliqué stitches.

> ### *Trusted Tip...*
> When working with silk, make sure your iron is on the appropriate setting for the fibre – the higher setting for cotton will scorch your silk!

Making the Patchwork

5 Add the patchwork borders to the circle blocks, using ¼in (6mm) seams. Begin with a partly sewn seam, stitching the first strip to the centre square but stopping after about 1½in (3.8cm) is stitched, as indicated by the green line in Fig 3A. Press all block seams outwards. Machine sew the next strip to the side of the block, as shown in Fig 3B. Continue adding strips until the block is complete, then finish the first seam, overlapping the stitches by about ½in (1.3cm). Make thirteen blocks this way.

A   B   C   D   E

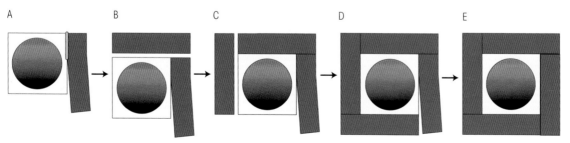

Fig 3

6 Make the chequerboard blocks using a Seminole patchwork technique as follows. Sew the strips together in sets of five as shown in Fig 4, with one orange and green set of 91in x 2½in (231.1cm x 6.4cm) strips, and the other green and orange set of 61in x 2½in (154.9cm x 6.4cm) strips. Press the seams towards the darker fabric. Cut each patchwork piece into 2½in (6.4cm) wide units, creating units of five sewn squares, as shown by the blue lines on the diagram. The length of the original strips is about ½in (1.3cm) longer than they need to be, to allow you to square up your ruler against the seams as you cut and trim off any excess, so the patchwork units are cut square across the strip. Cut thirty-six units with the orange squares at the ends and twenty-four with the green squares at the ends.

A

cut   strips 91in (231.1cm) long

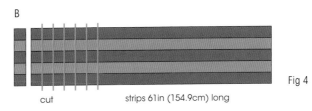

B

cut   strips 61in (154.9cm) long

Fig 4

7 Now rearrange and sew these units together as shown in Fig 5, to make twelve identical chequerboard blocks. Press these vertical seams towards the centre of the block.

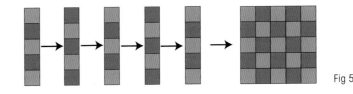

Fig 5

Assembling the Quilt Top

8 Lay out the blocks as shown in Fig 6, alternating the circle blocks and chequerboard blocks. Make sure the landscapes in the circles are the right way up. If you have pressed the block seams as described in the previous steps, the vertical seams on the chequerboard blocks will be pressed in the opposite direction to the border seams in the circle blocks, so the block seams will nest together neatly when the quilt top is assembled. Machine sew the blocks into columns and press horizontal seams towards the circle blocks.

Adding the Border

9 Machine sew the columns together to complete the quilt centre and press vertical seams towards the outside of the quilt. Machine sew the two 50½in x 1½in (128.3cm x 3.8cm) border strips across the top and bottom of the patchwork, and then add the two 52½in x 1½in (133.4cm x 3.8cm) strips on either side. Press the border strips outwards.

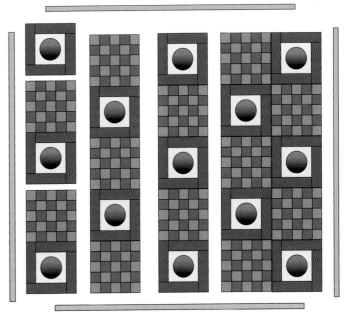

Fig 6

10 Machine sew on the wider border pieces, as shown in Fig 7, using the same part-sewn seam method used to add the borders to the circle blocks. Press seams towards the narrow quilt border, so it appears to be slightly raised above the wider outer border. Layer and tack (baste) the quilt ready for quilting, if quilting by hand or domestic machine – see Making a Quilt Sandwich.

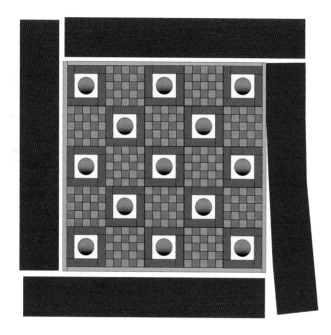

Fig 7

Quilting and Finishing

11 The quilt was free-hand quilted on a long-arm machine, with the machine guided by hand and designs 'drawn' with the needle. Different colours of thread are used to quilt different parts of the patchwork, achieving a subtle effect. The quilter took time to 'audition' threads by laying them over the quilt surface. The border design was inspired by the fronds of Japanese *sansai* (mountain vegetables) used in traditional farmhouse and Buddhist vegetarian cuisine. The pale background around the circles is quilted with a flame design but the circles themselves are not quilted, which throws them into relief, making them the quilt's main feature. If you wish to hand quilt this patchwork, stabilizing the top by stitching in the ditch along the patchwork seams would be a good starting point, perhaps adding some big stitch quilting along the circle block borders and outer border.

Trusted Tip...

If you plan to have your quilt long-arm quilted and intend to use silk, discuss this with your quilter in advance, as not all quilters may be happy working with this fibre. Some silks, such as Indian dupion, can be very rigid and papery with almost no stretch which can make it difficult to mount the quilt on the long-arm frame without putting some of the fabrics under a lot of stress. For the same reason, very fragile antique silks are best hand quilted.

12 Bind your quilt to finish – see Binding. Select a binding fabric to coordinate with your quilt, such as the black used here, which looks like a black lacquer frame. There's no need to match the border colour exactly and a slightly darker binding will help to frame the quilt.

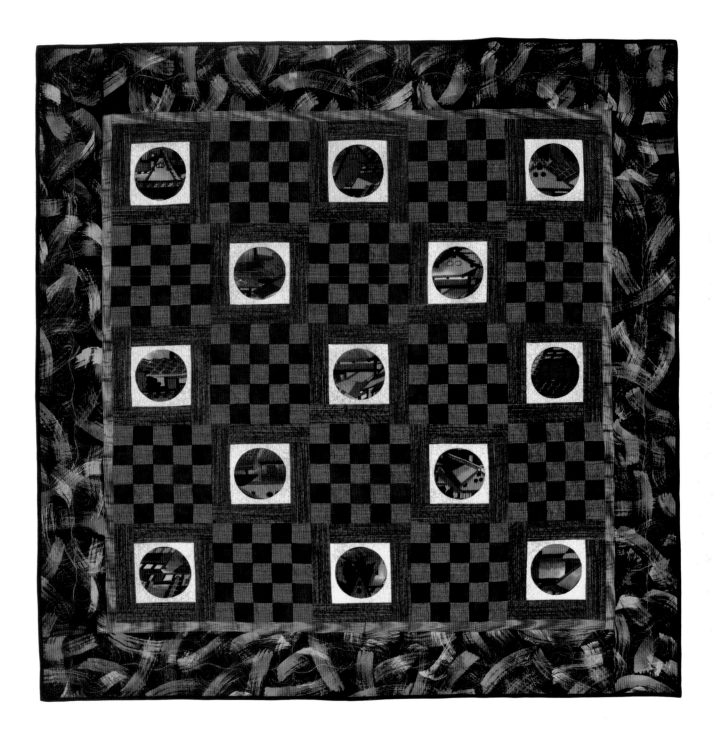

The timber frames and trim of traditional Japanese buildings just demand to be used in patchwork designs, as this quilt shows. Only seven fabrics were used for this quilt. The silk has great depth of colour, whether through the weave (the orange *tsumugi* in the blocks), an ombre effect (the green *tsumugi* in the chequerboards) or the glowing tiles and gables in the roofscape kimono fabric used for the circles. The subtleties of the hand dyed fabrics were enhanced by a careful choice of quilting threads and free-hand quilting, using the curled shapes of Japanese *sansai* (mountain vegetables), as inspiration for the border quilting designs.

Long-arm quilter: Ferret (see Suppliers)

Igeta
Well Curb

The *kanji* character *igeta* looks just like what it says, the criss-crossed timbers known as well-curbs which were once seen all over Japan, as a grille protecting the unwary from tumbling into an open well head. It has been a popular fabric motif for centuries, especially as a fashionably minimalist pattern on woven *kasuri* ikat cottons and for childrens' yukata cotton kimono.

An effective design for patchwork, the 10½in (26.7cm) blocks used here play with blending prints with the same plain colour to subtly merge the block border with the motif background. The thirty-six blocks make the quilt fat quarter friendly too, with each fat quarter making two *igeta* motifs, easily made using Seminole patchwork, and two block borders.

My friend's sons, Ryu and Ren, wear traditional boy's yukata to watch the Hanagasa Matsuri (Flower Hat Festival) procession, held annually in August in Yamagata City.

Fabric Focus

Look out for prints that share the same background colour, so the borders tend to blend with the background in each block. An exact colour match isn't necessary – slightly darker or lighter colours will work fine for some of the prints, but try to get a reasonable match with the others. Vary the scale and motifs in the prints. You could use a variety of plain cottons, matching the colour as closely as possible to each printed fabric.

Igeta Quilt

You will need

- Nine fat quarters with blue backgrounds
- Nine fat quarters with cream backgrounds
- ½yd (0.5m) of plain blue cotton, to match blue prints
- ½yd (0.5m) of plain cream cotton, to match cream prints
- Four 70½in x 7½in (179cm x 19cm) strips for border
- Sewing thread to tone with patchwork
- One skein of fine sashiko thread or No.12 perle or similar for big stitch quilting, beige thread for quilting border and red for tying block centres
- Backing fabric – see Wadding and Backing
- Wadding (batting) – see Wadding and Backing
- Binding fabric 320in (813cm) length

Finished quilt: 77in (195.5cm) square approximately

Cutting the Fabric

1 Cut fifty-four 6in x 2in (15.2cm x 5cm) pieces from each half yard/metre of plain fabric. Cut each fat quarter into eight 2in (5cm) wide strips, parallel to the selvedge, as shown in Fig 1, and sub-cut as follows. Cut eight 9½in x 2in (24.1cm x 5cm) strips for block borders (one from each strip), four 8in x 2in (20.3cm x 5cm) strips and four 6in x 2in (15.2cm x 5cm) strips.

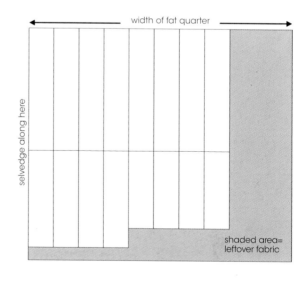

width of fat quarter

selvedge along here

shaded area=
leftover fabric

Fig 1

Sewing the Seminole Patchwork

2 Using ¼in (6mm) seams throughout, arrange and sew five 6in x 2in (15.2cm x 5cm) plain fabric strips together, alternating as shown in Fig 2. Press the seams towards the darker fabric.

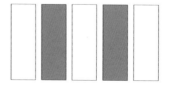

Fig 2

3 Now rotary cut each piece of patchwork into three 2in (5cm) wide slices as shown in Fig 3.

4 Arrange these patchwork strips with two 8in x 2in (20.3cm x 5cm) strips to make the block centres, matching the print fabric (Fig 4). Make thirty-six block centres in total, each measuring 8in (20.3cm) square.

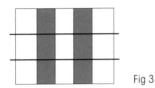

Fig 3

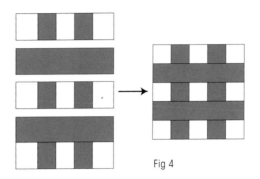

Fig 4

Trusted Tip. . .

When pressing the strips, pressing towards the darker fabric will prevent it shadowing through the paler one where pieces are joined. For hand quilting in the ditch, there is an added bonus – you will be mostly stitching on the paler fabric, so your work will be easier to see.

Assembling the Quilt Top

5 Using part-sewn seams and four 9½in x 2in (24.1cm x 5cm) strips per block, add a border to each block centre – see Sewing a Part-Sewn Seam. Blocks with cream backgrounds should have cream print borders and blocks with blue backgrounds should have blue print borders (Fig 5). Press towards the darker fabric. You can make the blocks as eighteen matching pairs or use a unique combination of fabrics in each block. For the two quilts in this chapter, the same combination of prints are used for four blocks – two blocks have light borders and two have dark borders, swapping the fabrics used for the *igeta* criss-cross centre in the block borders.

Fig 5

6 Arrange the blocks, alternating light and dark backgrounds until you are satisfied with the balance of the fabrics across the quilt, aiming for a random effect. Note that the long strips in each block centre *igeta* motif are horizontal (Fig 6). Sew blocks together in pairs to make rows and sew rows together in pairs to assemble the quilt top. Press seams towards the darker fabric.

Fig 6

Adding the Border

7 Measure your quilt top and cut fabric strips for the borders. Sew on the quilt borders using the same part-sewn seam technique used for the individual block borders (Fig 7). Press seams towards the quilt border.

Fig 7

Quilting and Finishing

8 Using your backing fabric and wadding (batting), layer and tack (baste) the quilt ready for quilting – see Making a Quilt Sandwich. The blue and white quilt is hand quilted in the ditch between the blocks, as shown in the photograph below (see also Hand Quilting). Each *igeta* criss-cross motif is quilted in the ditch. The centres of the motifs are tied with thick red cotton (see Tying a Quilt). Various threads are suitable, for example, coton à broder, fine sashiko thread or cotton perle No.12. Big stitch quilting is used in the border, with parallel lines about 2in (5cm) apart.

Trusted Tip. . .

Striped borders allow for very simple but effective quilting; simply follow some of the lines in the stripe, in the style of sashiko used for vintage Japanese work jackets. You can sew along a very narrow stripe or down the centre of a wider one. Using a contrasting thread will show off the stitching.

9 Bind your quilt to finish – see Binding. Select a binding fabric to coordinate with your quilt, such as the dark blue used here. There's no need to match the border colour exactly and a slightly darker binding will help to frame the quilt.

This quilt uses part-sewn seams to create a woven appearance to the block borders. As the patchwork design is so bold the quilting can be kept quite simple, with the blue and white version shown here hand quilted in the ditch around the motifs and tied with red thread at the block centres.

Matsuri Festival Quilt

This version of the Igeta Quilt uses a vibrant black and red colour scheme. In Japan, black and red are used together in many festival costumes and convey a happy feeling in this quilt. These colours are also popular shades for Japanese quilt fabrics, so sourcing nine of each isn't difficult, and they are easy colours to match for the plain backgrounds.

This quilt is made in exactly the same way as the blue and white version but with machine quilting instead of hand quilting. It was longarm machine quilted with black thread in a swirling pantograph design reminiscent of the way that water is depicted in Japanese art.

Long-arm quilter: Linda Paris (see Suppliers)

Yuza Taiko drum group perform wearing their traditional happi jackets at various festivals throughout the year.

A group of dancers at the Hanagasa Matsuri (Flower Hat Festival) in Yamagata City wearing traditional happi jackets, half red and half black. Dozens of groups attend from all over Yamagata Prefecture, each wearing their own distinctive colours.

Irori

Sunken Hearth

The *irori*, or sunken hearth, used to be the centre of family life in Japanese *minka* farmhouses. There was no chimney, so the smoke drifted out through the thatched roof. The *irori* survives today in the tea ceremony but uses charcoal. My 9in (22.9cm) quilt blocks have a central square to represent the hearth, with four rectangular patches going around it.

Combining stripes and other Japanese prints, the blocks are easy to make using part-sewn seams and 14½in (36.8cm) wide traditional Japanese fabrics can be included. Like Log Cabin blocks, they look effective with a bright centre square. The patchwork is arranged in strips, with each column stepping down by a third, giving a sense a movement. The quilt shown opposite uses early summer shades from a coordinated fat quarter pack, with two red prints for the block centres.

An iron kettle hangs over an *irori* at the Aoyama House, an unchanged nineteenth century fishing magnate's mansion near Yuza-machi. The lacquer box was used for carrying charcoal.

Fabric Focus

Fifteen fat quarters from a coordinated pack were used for the outer rectangles, with the two other fabrics, both red, used for the block centres. The same pattern is therefore repeated several times in different colours, giving unity to the quilt. The three extra block fabrics are all stripes, which add movement to the blocks. A fourth multicoloured stripe includes the touches of pink and green in the border. More stripes can be included if desired.

Irori Quilt

You will need

- Fifteen fat quarters of assorted prints
- Three fat quarters of striped fabric
- Two fat quarters or ½yd/0.5m for block centres
- Four 66½in x 3½in (168.9cm x 8.9cm) striped fabric strips for borders
- Sewing thread to tone with patchwork
- Quilting thread to contrast with patchwork (if machine quilting)
- Backing fabric to coordinate with patchwork – see Wadding and Backing
- Wadding (batting) – see Wadding and Backing
- Binding fabric 290in (737cm) length

Finished quilt: 69in (176.5cm) square approximately

Trusted Tip...

At slightly over 14in (35.5cm) wide, traditional Japanese cotton fabrics such as *yukata* cottons for summer kimono or slubbed *tsumugi* cottons are ideal for inclusion in this quilt design, as enough strips for three blocks can be cut very efficiently from a 19½in (49.5cm) length. The four border strips can also be cut from a 66½in (168.9cm) long piece of 14in (35.5cm) wide fabric.

Cutting the Fabric

1 There are forty-five complete blocks in the quilt. Each block needs one 3½in (8.9cm) centre square. Cut up to three sets of four strips 6½in x 3½in (16.5cm x 8.9cm) from each fat quarter. You will only need to cut two sets from several fat quarters, so select those fabrics you would like to feature most for the sets of three. Fig 1 shows how to cut these pieces from either a fat quarter or a piece of traditional narrow-width Japanese fabric.

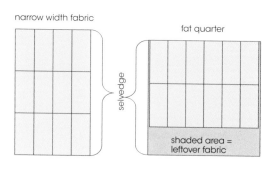

narrow width fabric

fat quarter

selvedge

shaded area = leftover fabric

Fig 1

2 Cut fifty-three 3½in (8.9cm) squares from the fabric selected for the block centres. There are four two-thirds blocks at the ends of four columns (see Fig 5). Each two-thirds block needs two 6½in x 3½in (16.5cm x 8.9cm) strips and one 3½in (8.9cm) square from the main fabrics plus one 3½in (8.9cm) centre square. A further twelve assorted squares are needed for the other ends of the same four columns. Cut these pieces from the fabric left over from cutting the main block strips. You may wish to choose the fabrics for these two-thirds blocks *after* making and arranging the full blocks.

Sewing the Patchwork Blocks

3 Using ¼in (6mm) seams throughout, arrange and machine sew forty-five blocks. Begin by making a partly sewn seam by stitching the first strip to the centre square but stopping after about 1½in (3.8cm) is stitched, as shown in Fig 2A and 2B and indicated by the blue line. Press the seam outwards. Machine sew the next strip to the side of the block, as shown in Fig 2C. Continue adding strips until the block is complete, then finish the first seam, overlapping the stitches by about ½in (1.3cm) (Figs 2D–F).

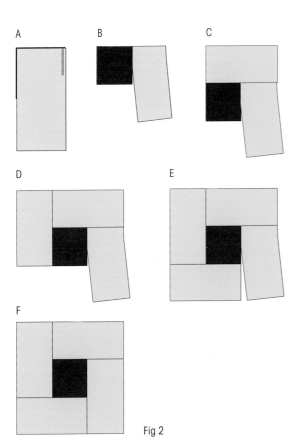

Fig 2

4 Machine sew the two-thirds blocks (there are four of these) as shown in Fig 3 and the four sets of three 3½in (8.9cm) squares, as shown in Fig 4.

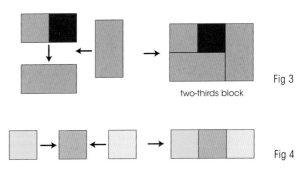

two-thirds block

Fig 3

Fig 4

Assembling the Quilt Top

5 Lay out the blocks as in Fig 5. There are no strict rules about which fabrics should go where, but if you have the same pattern in several colourways it looks better if these are spread out over the quilt rather than clustered in one area. Arrange the blocks until you are satisfied with the balance of the fabrics across the quilt, aiming for a random effect.

Fig 5

6 Sew the blocks together in vertical strips, as in Fig 5. Sew rows together in sequence to make the main panel. Because all the block seams are pressed towards the outside of each block, the seam allowances between the blocks will lie neatly in opposite directions when the strips are sewn together.

Quilting and Finishing

8 This version of the quilt is long-arm machine quilted using a pantograph pattern with a swirl motif, suggested by the quilter to harmonize with the water ripple patterns on some of the fabrics. As this quilt has an asymmetrical layout with a powerful diagonal emphasis, a quilting pattern that has a sense of movement rather than a rigid geometric pattern is more sympathetic to the quilt as a whole. Shaded thread adds a subtle touch.

9 Bind your quilt to finish – see Binding. Select a binding fabric to coordinate with your quilt, such as the dark blue I used. There's no need to match the border colour exactly and a slightly darker binding will help to frame the quilt.

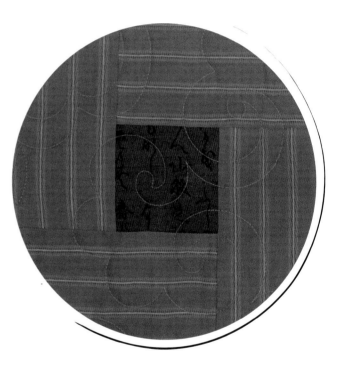

Adding the Border

7 Using your border strips, sew the border to the main quilt panel using the same part-sewn technique as for the blocks (Fig 6). Press seams towards the quilt border. Layer and tack (baste) the quilt ready for quilting, if quilting by hand or domestic machine – see Making a Quilt Sandwich.

Fig 6

Trusted Tip...

Computerized pantograph patterns for long-arm quilting include a wealth of motifs and your quilter will be able to find one that echoes elements in the fabric prints. Floral and abstract designs are particularly popular.

A restricted variety of pattern calls for careful placement of the blocks, in order that one pattern or colour doesn't dominate one area of the quilt – so every quilt will be unique. The mainly blue version at the end of this chapter has a larger proportion of stripes and geometric patterns. A long-arm pantograph pattern with swirls inspired by the ripples in one of the fabric patterns was used for the quilting.

Long-arm quilter: Linda Paris (see Suppliers)

Tatami Stripes Quilt

In this quilt, a higher proportion of striped fabrics makes the blocks look like tatami mats arranged around a *irori* hearth. Most of these fabrics are narrow width slubbed *tsumugi* cotton.

Sashiko-style big stitch quilting in fine cream sashiko thread reinforces the old-fashioned look. The quilting pattern is simple to mark using a 6in (15.2cm) diameter circle and half of the lines flow continuously across the quilt, forming a cross over the block centre, as shown in the diagram below. Before adding the big stitch, the quilt was hand quilted in the ditch between blocks and around the central squares.

Clothes like these were the everyday work wear of farming women in Yamagata Prefecture. Dark fabrics, many dyed with indigo, were preferred and it was believed that indigo strengthened the fibres. A little colour and pattern was introduced via stripes and kasuri ikat weaves. The cotton fabrics were often sashiko stitched for extra strength and warmth.

Shimacho

Fabric Scrapbook

Collecting fabrics is a passion quilters share with Japanese weavers and textile makers, who traditionally assembled their inspiration collections in scrapbooks called *shimacho* (stripe books). Various sizes of scraps, some just tiny fragments, would be pasted on to the pages in irregular arrangements. The idea makes a perfect scrap quilt, especially if mixing scrap sizes.

Each piece is bordered before being combined into nine 22in (55.9cm) blocks. Alternate blocks are rotated and sewn in a nine-patch arrangement. Using the part-sewn seam method to border each patch means seam allowances lie neatly in opposite directions or don't need to meet at all. The feature fabrics were emphasized by free-motion long-arm quilted meandering designs between patches. Seams are further camouflaged using a mini print for the border strips, so the patches seem to float on the background.

Displays of kimono fabrics often combine colours and patterns in exotic, almost clashing ways, with red being used as a 'neutral' colour in young women's kimono ensembles.

Traditional Japanese fabrics are sold in smaller pieces for patchwork and other handicrafts, often through specialist shops like Yuza-machi's Kasuriya.

Fabric Focus

You may already have pieces of Japanese fabrics left over from other patchwork projects which need using up. Strips can be cut down to make the smaller squares and the larger pieces include plenty of rectangles to make the most of what you have. Alternatively, you could use an assortment of fat quarters, 'eighths', 10in (25.4cm) squares or other pre-cut fabric selections. The narrow borders around each patch are pressed outwards, so the patches can include silks if you wish, which will be stabilized by the strip 'frame'.

Shimacho Quilt

You will need

- Assorted feature fabrics:
  A – fifty-four squares 2½in (6.4cm)
  B – eighteen squares 4½in (11.4cm)
  C – nine squares 6½in (16.5cm)
  D – twenty-seven strips 4½in x 2½in (11.4cm x 6.4cm)
  E – eighteen strips 6½in x 4½in (16.5cm x 11.4cm);
  F – nine strips 8½in x 6½in (21.6cm x 16.5cm);
  G – nine strips 10½in x 6½in (26.7cm x 16.5cm)

- Border fabric 3½yd (3.25m)

- Sewing thread to tone with patchwork

- Quilting thread to tone with patchwork (if machine quilting)

- Backing fabric to coordinate with patchwork – see Wadding and Backing

- Wadding (batting) – see Wadding and Backing

- Binding fabric to match border strips 290in (736.6cm) length approximately

Finished quilt: 68in (172.7cm) square approximately

Trusted Tip...

Although this is a fairly easy quilt to make, there are 144 feature fabric pieces and 576 border pieces (four for each feature fabric patch)! It is not as quick to make as some of the other quilts, so allow yourself plenty of time to piece it.

Cutting the Fabric

1 There are so many strips needed to border the feature fabric patches that it is easier to cut several sets at a time rather than attempting to cut all of them at once, when it is very easy to lose count and either cut too few or too many. The border strips can be sorted into piles with the relevant centre fabrics as you cut. Begin by cutting twenty or so 1½in (3.8cm) strips across the width of the border fabric.
Cut eighteen 9½in (24.1cm) and 11½in (29.2cm) strips and thirty-six 7½in (19cm) strips.
Each 10½in x 6½in (26.7cm x 16.5cm) piece needs two 11½in (29.2cm) and two 7½in (19cm) border strips.
Each 8½in x 6½in (21.6cm x 16.5cm) piece needs two 9½in (24.1cm) and two 7½in (19cm) border strips. The shorter pieces left over from cutting the longer pieces can be used when you cut the borders for the 2½in (6.4cm) squares.

2 Continue cutting strips for the medium-sized rectangular patches. Cut thirty-six 7½in (19cm) strips, fifty-four 3½in (8.9cm) strips and ninety 5½in (14cm) strips.
Each 6½in x 4½in (16.5cm x 11.4cm) piece needs two 7½in (19cm) and two 5½in (14cm) border strips.
Each 4½in x 2½in (11.4cm x 6.4cm) piece needs two 5½in (14cm) and two 3½in (8.9cm) strips.

3 Cut the border strips for the squares. Cut thirty-six 7½in (19cm) strips for the 6½in (16.5cm) square borders, seventy-two 5½in (14cm) strips for the 4½in (11.4cm) squares and 216 strips 3½in (8.9cm) long for the 2½in (6.4cm) squares. Keep the remaining fabric to make the long borders on the outside of the quilt.

Sewing the Patchwork Blocks

4 Using ¼in (6mm) seams throughout, arrange and machine sew the blocks with the 6½in (16.5cm) square patches first. Begin by making a partly sewn seam by stitching the first strip to the centre square but stopping after about 1½in (3.8cm) (indicated by the red line in Fig 1A). Press the seam outwards. Machine sew the next strip to the side of the block. Continue adding strips until the block is complete, then finish the first seam, overlapping the stitches by about ½in (1.3cm).

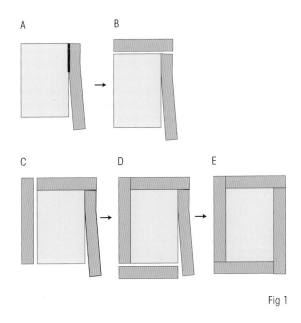

Fig 1

Trusted Tip...

If you have not sewn a block with part-sewn seams before, begin with one of the larger, square blocks and work your way down to the smaller squares, where the seams are shorter and the space to fit the sewing machine foot into the patchwork seam is slightly less.

5 Machine sew the other blocks with square centre patches, then sew the blocks with the rectangular centre patches. You will need to check that you are sewing the longer border strip side to the *longest* side of the patch each time – it is easy to get mixed up and sew a short border piece to the longer patch side. Once all the block borders are added, you can arrange and assemble the larger blocks.

Assembling the Quilt Top

6 Lay out the all the pieces for each of the larger blocks as shown in Fig 2. Each 22in (55.9cm) square block is comprised of the following smaller units (shown within the dotted boxes on the diagram). These are, listed by block centre patch size – six A 2½in (6.4cm) squares, two B 4½in (11.4cm) squares, one C 6½in (16.5cm) square, three D 4½in x 2½in (11.4cm x 6.4cm) units, two E 6½in x 4½in (16.5cm x 11.4cm) units, one F 8½in x 6½in (21.6cm x 16.5cm) unit and one G 10½in x 6½in (26.7cm x 16.5cm) unit.

7 Machine sew the smaller units together to make the larger ones. Begin by sewing the 2½in (6.4cm) centre blocks together. Press seams in the directions indicated by the red arrows so the seam allowances in adjacent blocks (in the few places where they meet) will lie in opposite directions, enabling the patchwork seams to butt up together snugly. The finished large block should look like Fig 3.

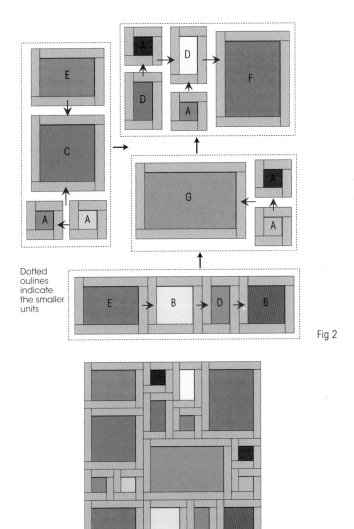

Dotted oulines indicate the smaller units

Fig 2

Fig 3

8 All nine larger blocks are identical, but alternate blocks are turned upside down to create the finished quilt pattern. Lay out the large blocks as shown in Fig 5. The blocks in the corners and the centre of the quilt stay the right way up but turn the other four upside down, achieving the patchwork's random look. Machine sew the blocks into columns, pressing the joining seams in opposite directions, and then sew the columns together to make the quilt centre.

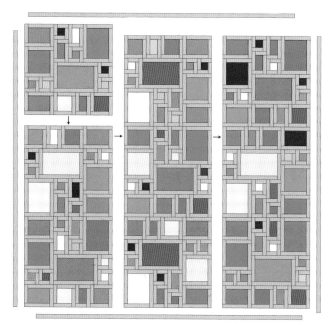

Fig 4

Adding the Border

9 Measure your quilt, down and across before cutting 1½in (3.8cm) wide fabric strips across the fabric width for the narrow border. The quilt border pieces are added using the same part-sewn seam method as the smaller block borders. Mine measured 67½in (171.4cm), the length of one side of the patchwork plus 1in (2.5cm) overlap at the corners. Two strips will need to be joined for each border. If you prefer, sew on each border and trim to length after sewing; for a single narrow border this should not make the quilt edge wavy as it would for multiple borders. Press seams towards the border. Layer and tack (baste) the quilt ready for quilting, if quilting by hand or domestic machine – see Making a Quilt Sandwich.

Quilting and Finishing

10 Free-hand long-arm quilting allows the quilter to follow the asymmetrical piecing with the quilting design, so the feature fabrics appear a little more three-dimensional in the quilting. A meandering design in the borders helps to emphasize the feature fabrics and disguises the seams between the patches, focusing the viewer's attention on all the lovely prints. If you want to make more of a feature of the block borders, try using different shades of the same colour on adjacent blocks, such as mixing dark indigo blues and perhaps quilting along the centre of each strip or in the ditch around the block centres to emphasize the border strips.

11 Bind your quilt to finish – see Binding. If you use the same fabric for the block borders and binding, it will be almost invisible.

A collection of different sized pieces of fabric make the perfect scrap quilt. Here, the smallest piece is 2½in (6.4cm) square and the largest 10½in x 6½in (26.7cm x 16.5cm). Very few fabrics are used only once, but the asymmetric arrangement of the patches fools the eye into thinking this is a true scrap quilt. A free-hand meander was quilted across the border strips, leaving the fabric collection to be the main focus.

Long-arm quilter: Maria Laza (see Suppliers)

Sensu

Fan

Fans are one of the objects most people immediately associate with Japan and they are indispensable accessories during the humid summer months. The paper folding fan or *sensu* is often used as a decorative motif and the elegant arched shape of the fan papers frequently function as a picture outline – the ideal place to showcase some of my favourite cotton *yukata* kimono fabrics.

The 8in (20.3cm) fan block is easy to make using machine sewn freezer paper appliqué. The vertical panels between blocks are roughly a third of the width of commercial patchwork fabrics, so either can be used. It was free-hand quilted on a long-arm machine using a simple meander to give extra dimension to the delightful farmhouse and hills motif on the *yukata* fabrics.

In Japan, the annual display of the latest cotton yukata fabrics and yukata accessories heralds the summer in kimono shops. Whether your taste is for traditional blue and white or something more contemporary, the bold yukata fabrics give a cheerful, relaxed feeling. Yukata are worn informally at summer festivals.

Fabric Focus

While large-scale fabrics are suitable for the fans, other fabrics can be included, such as tiny blue and white prints. Take time to select the most interesting parts of your fabrics for the fans, remembering that designs don't need to be placed symmetrically. The shape of the rice ear design on the purple fabric echoes the curve of the fan, as does the sunflower. The rabbit designs were too cute not to include. The diagonally patterned faux *shibori* (tie dye) background zigzags behind the fans for extra movement.

Sensu Quilt

You will need

- For the fan blocks:
  sixteen 8½in (21.6cm) squares for
  backgrounds and sixteen assorted
  pieces at least 9½in x 5in (24.1cm x
  12.7cm) for fans

- Three 64½in (163.8cm) strips of
  yukata cotton, each 14in–15in
  (35.5cm–38.1cm) wide
  or one 64½in (163.8cm) length of
  patchwork cotton, cut into three 14in
  (35.5cm) wide strips (see step 5)

- Freezer paper to make appliqué
  templates (on a roll type)

- Sewing thread to tone with patchwork

- Quilting thread to contrast with
  patchwork (if machine quilting)

- Backing fabric to coordinate with
  patchwork – see Wadding and
  Backing

- Wadding (batting) – see Wadding and
  Backing

- Binding fabric 260in (660cm) length

Finished quilt: 64in (162.5cm) long x up to 58in
(147.3cm) wide (with yukata/kimono fabric)

Trusted Tip...

Half the fan blocks will be rotated by
90 degrees, so think carefully if using a
directional fabric for the background or
a stripe as it will be on its side in half the
blocks. If the background fabric is abstract
with diagonal bands, like the faux *shibori* print
here, this can make an interesting zigzag
effect. If using a landscape print, it would
need to be the right way up in each block.

Cutting the Fabric

1 Trace off sixteen freezer paper fan outlines from the fan
template opposite. Using the iron on a cool setting, iron each
template on to the back of a piece of the fan fabric, arranging the
fans so that attractive motifs are framed by the fans. Cut out the
fans, allowing a generous ¼in–⅜in (6mm–1cm) hem allowance
on the curves but none along the straight sides, as shown in Fig
1. The seam allowances on the straight sides are included in the
template and the dashed lines show where the ends of the fan
will be sewn into the patchwork seams.

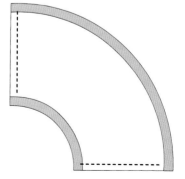

Fig 1

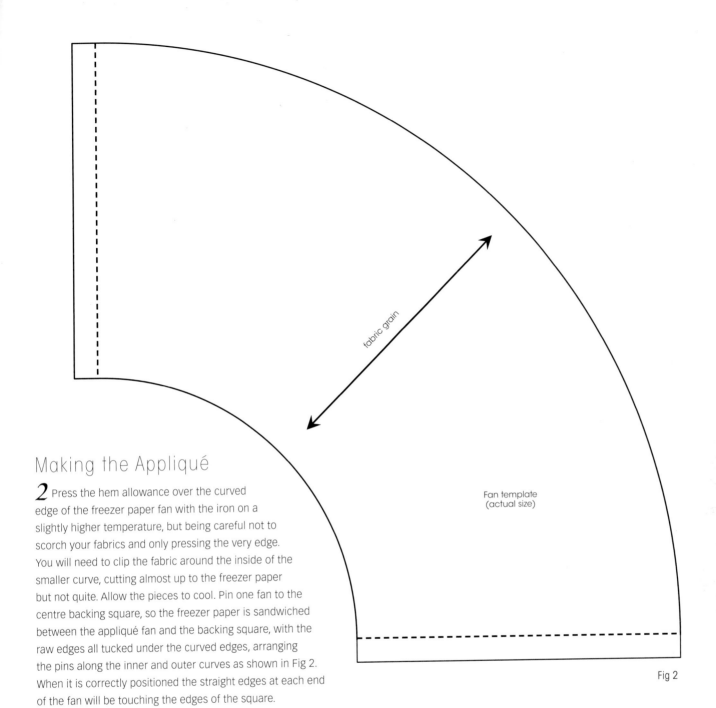

fabric grain

Fan template
(actual size)

Fig 2

Making the Appliqué

2 Press the hem allowance over the curved
edge of the freezer paper fan with the iron on a
slightly higher temperature, but being careful not to
scorch your fabrics and only pressing the very edge.
You will need to clip the fabric around the inside of the
smaller curve, cutting almost up to the freezer paper
but not quite. Allow the pieces to cool. Pin one fan to the
centre backing square, so the freezer paper is sandwiched
between the appliqué fan and the backing square, with the
raw edges all tucked under the curved edges, arranging
the pins along the inner and outer curves as shown in Fig 2.
When it is correctly positioned the straight edges at each end
of the fan will be touching the edges of the square.

3 The appliqué can be hand or machine sewn to the backing
square – see Appliqué. Do not sew across the straight ends of
the fans (Fig 3). Turn each block over and carefully cut away the
background fabric, leaving a generous ¼in (6mm) allowance
behind each fan. Remove the freezer paper by peeling it away
from the back of the fans. Gently scrunching up the paper along
the fan edges will help loosen it from the appliqué stitches.
Appliqué fans to all sixteen blocks.

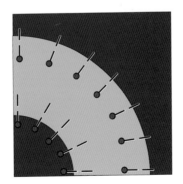

Fig 3

Making the Patchwork

4 Lay out the fan blocks into two columns of eight blocks each, turning half the blocks through 90 degrees, as shown in Fig 4. The placement of the different fans is very much a matter of personal taste and a random arrangement works best. Once you are happy with the block layout, machine sew them together in pairs using a ¼in (6mm) seam allowance and sew the pairs together to make two columns of eight blocks each. Press the seam allowances downwards.

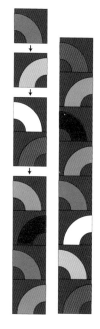

Fig 4

Assembling the Quilt Top

5 Arrange the patchwork strips between the three 64½in (163.8cm) long strips (Fig 5). (Note: patchwork fabric 42in–44in (106.7cm–111.7cm) wide can be cut into three 14in (35.5cm) wide strips and used instead of *yukata* cotton, but the finished quilt will be slightly narrower.) The pattern repeat will be in a slightly different position on each long strip, so move the three strips around until you are happy with the sequence. This is particularly important if you have three strips cut from patchwork fabric, as the pattern may look odd if it continues very obviously on either side of the fan patchwork strip. Machine sew the columns together to complete the quilt centre and press vertical seams towards the long strips, away from the patchwork.

Fig 5

Quilting and Finishing

6 Layer and tack (baste) the quilt ready for quilting, if quilting by hand or domestic machine – see Making a Quilt Sandwich. Free-motion long-arm quilting was chosen for this quilt because the beautiful stencilled vintage *yukata* cotton had a design worth emphasizing, rather than using a pantograph design down each yukata strip – an option that would work well with many fabrics. The quilter experimented with ideas on smaller samples and decided to add some extra quilting to the landscape *yukata* cotton, to bring out the shapes of the farmhouses.

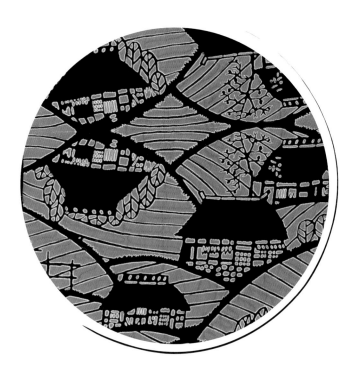

Trusted Tip...

If you have some spare fabrics or blocks and would like a hand-guided design for your quilt, ask your quilter if they could use them, as you will be able to get a very good impression of how the quilting will work. Feel free to discuss your ideas with your quilter – a good professional quilter will welcome input.

7 Bind your quilt to finish – see Binding. Select a fabric to coordinate with your quilt, such as the dark blue used here. A slightly darker binding can frame the quilt and also looks better against the ends of the fan block strips.

Rotating alternate fan blocks in this quilt gives a lively feeling to the design, almost like fans fluttering. A controlled colour palette for the background and strip fabrics contrasts with the often very colourful fans. Although the fans don't have appliquéd sticks, each gives the impression of the fan frame through the quilting design. The wide strips between the blocks are the perfect place to display a really beautiful fabric that will benefit from being kept in large sections. The rounded hills and the tiny farmhouses nestling among them have been emphasized with the quilting design.

Long-arm quilter: Maria Laza (see Suppliers)

Kamigata Bunka Quilt

Trade with Kyoto brought sophisticated *Kamigata* culture to Yamagata Prefecture during the Edo era and festivals like the *Hina Matsuri* (doll festival) are celebrated in the old capital's style. The ornamental dolls, representing the Imperial court, are displayed on a tiered stand. The chance discovery of a print featuring the Hina dolls and another with temple rooftops, both heavily overprinted with gold, suggested this combination. The rich purple and gold background for the fans includes patterns once used for aristocratic clothing.

Sashiko-style big stitch in red coton à broder echoes the fan outlines, which were also hand quilted in the ditch. Quilting follows the curves of the roofs across the fabric strips.

My friend's daughter showed me her Hina Dolls in their storage boxes at New Year, although the Hina Matsuri is celebrated on the third day of the third month. The memory of this suggested including pine and plum motifs, associated with New Year, for some of the applique fans in this quilt.

Magnificent temple architecture can be found all over Japan. The upturned eaves of the gate at the Honmonji temple in Tokyo are typical of the temple roofs captured in the main quilt fabric.

Masu
Measuring Boxes

The simplicity of a square in a square is used in this lovely quilt, echoing the pattern formed by *masu*, stacking boxes once used to measure rice. The quilt is arranged with 14in (35.5cm) blocks, which provide ample space for using 2½in (6.4cm) wide pre-cut fabric strips to great effect. Forty strips, the number most frequently sold in strip packs, are just enough to make sixteen blocks with a great variety of colours and tones.

The quilt is a reflection of early summer, with its light green, pale blue, brown, off-white and burnt orange colours. Fabric patterns range from contemporary interpretations of traditional patterns, like *tatewaku* (rising steam) and dragonfly motifs, to retro concentric circles and tiny leaves. The quilt was long-arm quilted with a pantograph dragonfly pattern.

The colours of the summer countryside in northern Japan inspired this quilt — the fresh green of rice fields, flashes of orange flowers where dragonflies alight after showers, the mellow brown of an old barn…

Fabric Focus

A fully coordinated pack of pre-cut 2½in (6.4cm) wide strips takes the work out of fabric selection. Some are produced by fabric manufacturers but many quilt shops cut their own. Most packs have forty different fabrics, while others may include some duplicates, which will be useful for this design. If your pack has fewer strips, purchase some thin quarters or half yards of coordinating fabrics and cut extra strips yourself.

Masu Quilt

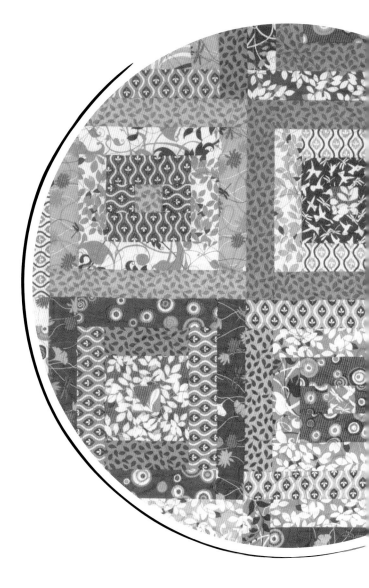

You will need

- Forty fabric strips 2½in x 42in–44in (6.4cm x 106.7cm–111.7cm)

- Border fabric: two strips each 56½in x 7½in (143.5cm x 19cm) and two strips each 70in x 7½in (177.8cm x 19cm)

- Sewing thread to tone with patchwork

- Quilting thread to contrast with patchwork (if machine quilting)

- Backing fabric to coordinate with patchwork – see Wadding and Backing

- Wadding (batting) – see Wadding and Backing

- Binding fabric 300in (762cm) length

Finished quilt: 70in (177.8cm) square approximately

Cutting the Fabric

1 Thirty-two strips in sixteen pairs are needed for the outer and middle 'boxes' in the blocks. Pair any identical strips and select other pairs from similar fabrics, e.g., two green background prints or two prints with similar amounts of blue and white. Cut two strips 14½in (36.8cm) and two strips 6½in (16.5cm) from the first strip in each pair, as shown in Fig 1. Cut four 10½in (26.7cm) strips from the second strip in each pair. The outer 'box' uses two 14½in (36.8cm) and two 10½in (26.7cm) strips; the middle 'box' uses two 10½in (26.7cm) and two 6½in (16.5cm) strips.

2 Cut the centre squares and the inner 'boxes' as follows. From each of the eight remaining strips cut four 6½in (16.5cm) strips and six 2½in (6.4cm) squares, as shown in Fig 2.

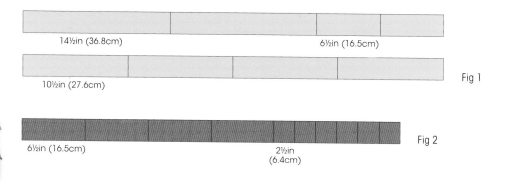

14½in (36.8cm)   6½in (16.5cm)

10½in (27.6cm)

Fig 1

6½in (16.5cm)   2½in (6.4cm)

Fig 2

Sewing the Patchwork Blocks

3 Using ¼in (6mm) seams throughout, arrange and sew sixteen blocks as in Fig 3. Use a different fabric for the centre square and the inner 'box' each time. Sew two 2½in (6.4cm) squares on the opposite sides of the centre square, then sew two matching 6½in (16.5cm) strips to the other sides (Fig 3A). Add the next set of strips to make the next box. The strips used for each box should be either the same fabric or a very similar colour match, i.e., the shorter strips can be one fabric and the longer strips another, with two fabrics used instead of one, but they should look similar. Try to alternate light and dark sets of strips. Press all seams towards the outside of the block.

Trusted Tip...

With no two identical blocks in this quilt, their arrangement is a matter of personal taste. Try taking a series of snapshots of different layouts, as this may help you decide the best arrangement for your blocks.

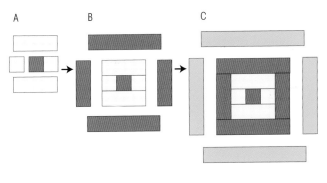

A   B   C

Fig 3

5 Sew the blocks together in pairs to make strips (see Fig 4), pressing seams towards unpieced edges of the blocks. Sew strips together in pairs to assemble the quilt top, pressing these seams towards the outside of the quilt.

Trusted Tip...

Arrange the strips in each block before sewing, making sure you like the combination of fabrics in each. The quilt looks best if no two blocks have exactly the same combination of fabrics in the same strip positions.

Assembling the Quilt Top

4 Lay out the blocks as shown in Fig 4. Try alternating between light and dark outer 'boxes' in each block. Blocks with darker outer border fabrics are best placed at the bottom corners of the quilt, so the design doesn't look top heavy. Note that alternate blocks are rotated 90 degrees, so the long strips on the side of each block will be against the seamed side of the next block and there is no need to match up seams at the block edges. Arrange the blocks until you are satisfied with the balance of the fabrics across the quilt, aiming for a random effect.

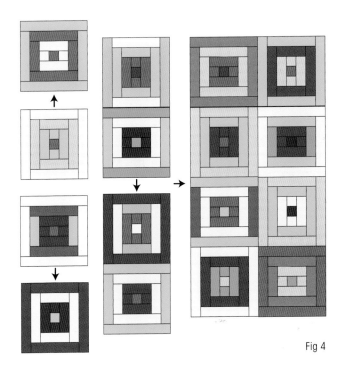

Fig 4

Adding the Border

6 Measure your quilt top and cut fabric strips for the borders, following the advice in Adding a Border. Sew on the top and bottom borders first, and then add the longer side borders. Press seams towards the quilt border. Layer and tack (baste) the quilt ready for quilting, if quilting by hand or domestic machine – see Making a Quilt Sandwich.

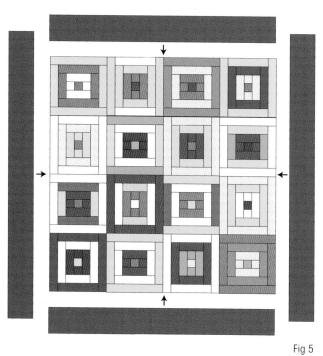

Fig 5

Quilting and Finishing

7 The quilt shown opposite was long-arm machine quilted using a pantograph pattern featuring dragonflies connected by loops and curves, suggesting their flight patterns. This design was selected because it repeated the dragonfly motif featured on some of the fabric prints. An asymmetrical pattern with plenty of curves can be a good choice for a quilt with very bold geometric patchwork, as the design can flow easily across the quilt surface without needing to line up with the patchwork blocks.

8 Bind your quilt to finish – see Binding. Select a binding fabric to coordinate with your quilt, such as the dark brown I used. There's no need to match the border colour exactly and a slightly darker binding will help to frame the quilt.

Trusted Tip...

The beige quilting thread makes the quilting almost invisible against some fabrics but brings the quilting pattern to the fore against darker fabrics and the striped border. An off-white thread, the same colour as in the print background, would have seemed too pale and harsh once quilted. Take time to find the best colour for your quilting thread by unwinding a length and laying it over the quilt top.

In this quilt no two blocks have exactly the same fabric combination and placement so, although there are only sixteen blocks, the variety of colours and tones can seem like abstract art. In addition, the 2½in (6.4cm) wide strips are wide enough to reveal the fabric print. A pantograph dragonfly pattern was long-arm quilted, echoing the dragonfly print.

Long-arm quilter: Linda Paris (see Suppliers)

Tsuyu Summer Quilt

This quilt captures the mood of the rainy season in Japan. A roll of 2½in (6.4cm) wide strips was the starting point for a tranquil colour scheme of greenish-blues and lilacs with a metallic gold shimmer. Because the roll had only thirty strips, ten more were cut from a couple of ½yd (0.5m) pieces, so some fabrics appear more often than others.

The swirl fabric in the border was left over from the Kimono Quilt, so the borders had to be narrower, reducing the size to 60in (152.4cm) square. A pantograph pattern was used for the long-arm machine quilting, using the flowers in the fabrics and a continuous-line quilting motif. To hand quilt, quilting in the ditch would suffice, making the nested squares the quilting design as well as the patchwork pattern. The block centres could be tied – see Tying a Quilt.

Long-arm quilter: Linda Paris (see Suppliers)

These Chinese bellflowers were growing by a massive rock feature at the Teien, a private garden near Yuza-machi. Their delicate bells are often depicted as one of the 'akikusa' or autumn herbs. Their colour adds a cool feeling with a hint of approaching autumn to the summer scene.

In Japan hydrangeas bloom at the start of the rainy season in late June. The refreshing blue flower heads make bold motifs for cotton yukata, casual summer kimono.

Sakiori

Rag Weave

Colourful *sakiori* is woven from strips of recycled fabrics, fragmenting colours and patterns into a tweedy texture. This was made into obi sashes, work clothes, floor cushions and rugs. Cotton warps in different colours were often added for a plaid effect.

This striped effect is recreated by using 1½in (3.8cm) wide strips throughout this quilt, so it is ideal for narrow pre-cut strip rolls. Piecing long strips together before cutting into 8½in (21.6cm) squares is quick to do. The patchwork effect of *sakiori* is emphasized by the asymmetric block arrangement, which is broken up by appliquéd circle and square-in-a-square blocks. It was machine quilted with *marumon* (circular motifs) and an all-over pattern resembling *sakiori's* coloured warp threads. The bright pastels of these fabrics remind me of the paper strips that decorate 'trees' during the Tanabata festival.

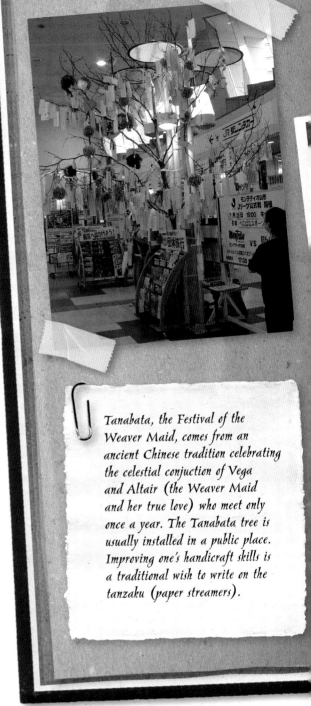

Tanabata, the Festival of the Weaver Maid, comes from an ancient Chinese tradition celebrating the celestial conjuction of Vega and Altair (the Weaver Maid and her true love) who meet only once a year. The Tanabata tree is usually installed in a public place. Improving one's handicraft skills is a traditional wish to write on the tanzaku (paper streamers).

Fabric Focus

At least eighty 43in–44in x 1½in (109.2cm–111.8cm x 3.8cm) strips are needed, the equivalent of two 1½in (3.8cm) pre-cut strip rolls, so five 8½in (21.6cm) squares can be cut from each patchwork strip. If only four squares can be cut, sixteen more strips will be needed. The overall effect is that of a scrap quilt and the finished strips are only 1in (2.5cm) wide, so the fabric patterns are a secondary feature to the overall colour scheme.

Sakiori Quilt

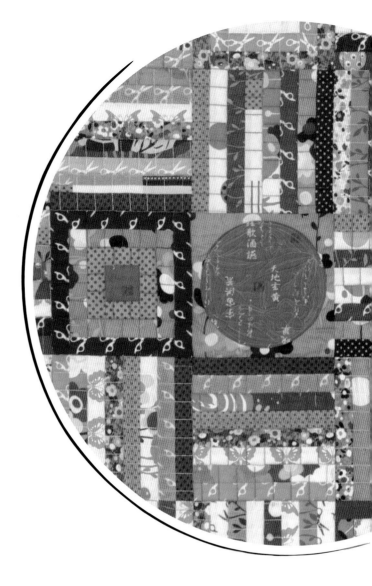

You will need

- Eighty strips 1½in x 43in–44in (3.8cm x 109.2cm–111.8cm)

- Seven assorted 8½in (21.6cm) squares

- Fabric for appliqué circles ½yd (0.5m)

- Fabric for border (could be pieced):
  two strips 64½in x 1½in (163.8cm x 3.8cm)
  two strips 58½in x 1½in (148.6cm x 3.8cm)

- Seven 7in (17.8cm) diameter freezer paper circles

- Sewing thread to tone with patchwork

- Quilting thread

- Backing fabric – see Wadding and Backing

- Wadding (batting) – see Wadding and Backing

- Binding fabric 276in (700cm) length

Finished quilt: 66½in x 58½in
(168.9cm x 148.6cm) approximately

Cutting the Fabric

1 For the circle block centres, use the iron on a cool setting to iron the seven freezer paper circles on to the back of the ½yd (0.5m) fabric piece. Cut out the circles, cutting a generous ¼in (6mm) away from the edge of the paper, to allow for the appliqué hem, as shown in Fig 1. Cut nine 2½in (6.4cm) squares from the remaining fabric, for the square-in-a-square block centres.

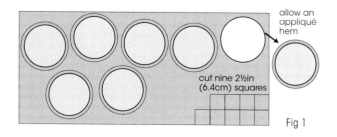

allow an appliqué hem

cut nine 2½in (6.4cm) squares

Fig 1

2 Select sixteen of the full-width strips for the square-in-a-square blocks, including as many pairs of strips as possible (easy if you are using two identical pre-cut packs). There are nine of these blocks. Cut the following for each block, starting with the longest strips (A) and removing the selvedge at the end.

A – two 8½in (21.6cm) strips and two 6½in (16.5cm) strips
   (30in/76.2cm total).

B – two 6½in (16.5cm) strips and two 4½in (11.4cm) strips
   (22in/55.9cm total).

C – two 4½in (11.4cm) strips and two 2½in (6.4cm) strips
   (13in/33cm total).

Trusted Tip...

One set of A strips and one set of C strips can be cut if strips measure 44in (111.8cm) but not if the strips are only 43in (109.2cm). How economically these strips can be cut will depend on the depth of the selvedge. Cut extra strips from the circle leftovers if necessary.

Making the Appliqué

3 Press the hem allowance over the edge of the freezer paper circles with the iron on a slightly higher temperature, but being careful not to scorch your fabrics and only pressing the very edge. Allow the pieces to cool. Pin one circle to the centre backing square, so the freezer paper is sandwiched between the appliqué circle and the backing square, with the raw edges all tucked under, arranging the pins as shown in Fig 2. You can check it is central by measuring the space between the edges of the circle and the sides of the square, which should be approximately ¾in (1.9cm).

4 The appliqué can be hand or machine sewn to the backing square – see Appliqué. Once finished, cut a vertical slit behind the circle, taking care not to cut the circle itself, and remove the freezer paper by scrunching it up and pulling it out through the slit. Scrunching up the fabric a little around the circle helps to loosen the paper where it may have been caught by the appliqué stitches.

Sewing the Strip Patchwork

5 Arrange the remaining strips into eight sets of eight, contrasting rather than coordinating neighbouring strips. Using ¼in (6mm) seams throughout, arrange and sew eight strips together as shown in Fig 3. Sew the strips in pairs, then sew pairs together. Starting from the end opposite the printed selvedge each time, so the ends of the strips will all line up at one end – the other end will be slightly staggered. Keep seam allowances even, especially at the ends of the seams. You may prefer to piece these using a walking foot. Press all the seams in the same direction.

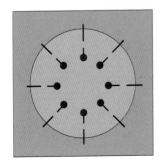

Fig 2

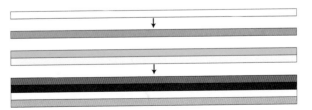

Fig 3

6 Rotary cut each piece of patchwork into five 8½in (21.6cm) squares as shown by the red lines in Fig 4A. It is a tight squeeze to get five squares out of the patchwork width, so cut as economically as you can. Begin by trimming off ¼in (6mm) from the straightest end, leaving a little of the printed selvedge on the strip – this will disappear into a patchwork seam. Make sure you are cutting the squares accurately, with the patchwork seams parallel to the ruler (Fig 4B).

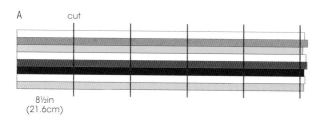

Fig 4

Sewing the Square-in-a-Square Blocks

7 Using the strips cut previously in step 2 and ¼in (6mm) seams throughout, arrange and sew the block as shown in Fig 5. Sew two 2½in (6.4cm) strips on the opposite sides of the centre square first, then sew two matching 4½in (11.4cm) strips to the other sides. Continue sewing the block by adding the next set of strips to make the next square. The strips for each square should match. Try alternating light and dark sets of strips. Press all seams towards the outside of the block. Make nine blocks in total.

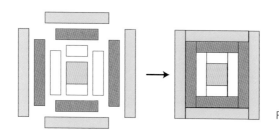

Fig 5

Assembling the Quilt Top

8 Arrange the blocks as shown in Fig 6 opposite. Place the circle blocks first, then position the square-in-a-square blocks. Fill in with the strip blocks. Try to achieve a random block arrangement, so avoid having the same strip sequence in adjacent blocks. Note how some of the blocks have the strips running vertically while others are horizontal.

Trusted Tip...

Swap blocks around until you are happy with their arrangement. Taking reference photos can help.

9 Machine sew the blocks together, using Fig 6 as a guide. The blocks are assembled in groups, indicated by the dotted line boxes behind the blocks. The green arrows show the direction for pressing the joining seams, so that the finished block joining seams will be pressed in opposite directions. This means that the seam allowances will fit together neatly. The seams between the blocks are also pressed away from the pieced edge where possible to make the seams less bulky, but note there are a few places where it is necessary to press towards the block edge with the most seams. Where the strip blocks meet a square-in-a-square block, it will occasionally be necessary to flip one of the strip block seam allowances the opposite way.

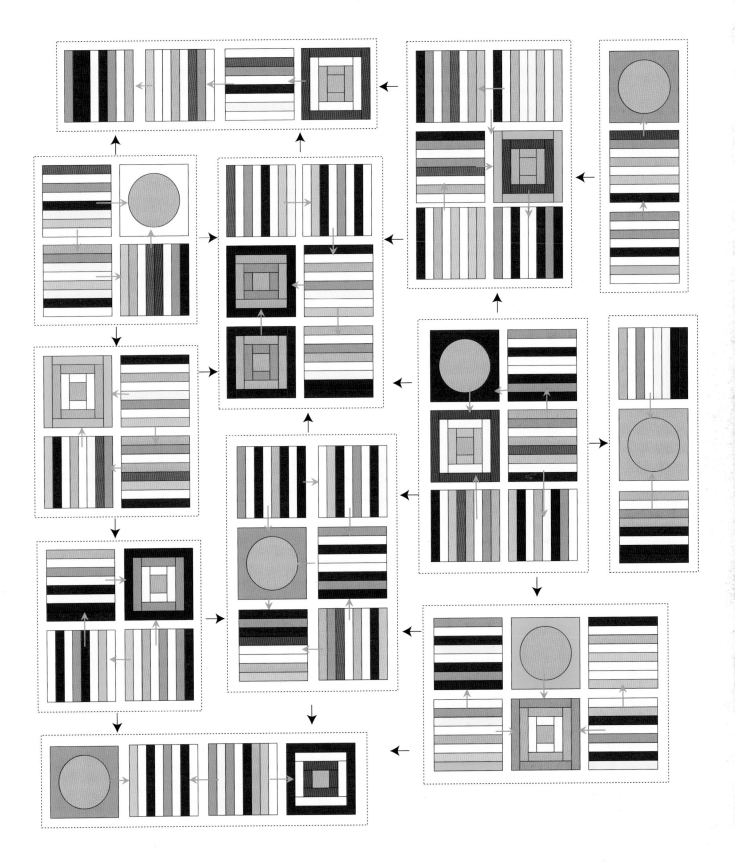

Fig 6

Adding the Border

10 The narrow border is simply added to provide a stable edge to the patchwork and may be omitted if you prefer. Measure your quilt top and cut fabric strips for the borders, following the advice in Adding a Border. As there are so many seams in this patchwork, the centre panel may measure slightly less than anticipated, so the border can be trimmed to fit. Sew on the side borders first, then sew the top and bottom borders. Press seams towards the quilt border. Layer and tack (baste) the quilt ready for quilting – see Making a Quilt Sandwich.

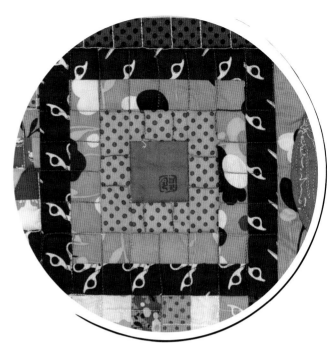

Fig 7

12 Bind your quilt to finish – see Binding. Select a binding fabric to coordinate with your quilt. There's no need to match the border colour exactly. The red binding has a linear design of leaves and was included in the patchwork. To retain the pattern, the binding was cut on the crosswise fabric grain, not on the bias.

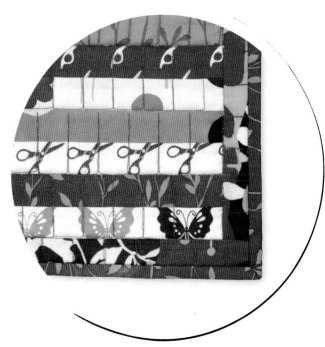

Quilting and Finishing

11 The quilt shown opposite was long-arm machine quilted, guided by computer. The quilter used a selection of circular Japanese motifs and scaled these to fit the appliqué circles. Each circle has a different *marumon* (circular motif). The straight line quilting over the strip blocks is actually a U-shaped pattern, designed especially for this quilt. Brick red and white threads were used to quilt different areas, giving the effect of the coloured cotton warp threads often used for woven *sakiori*.

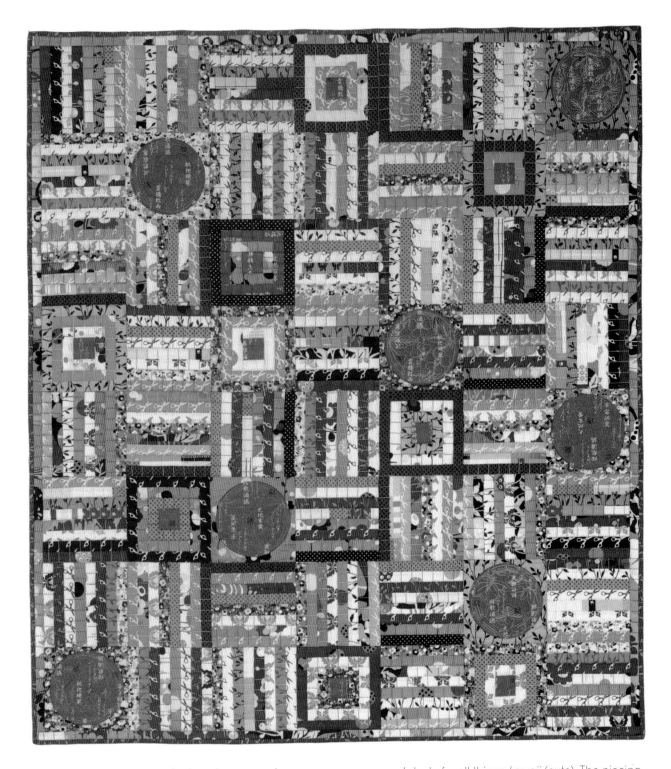

Colourful modern prints reflect contemporary Japanese young women's taste for all things *kawaii* (cute). The piecing echoes the strippy effect of *sakiori* rag weave, while the circular appliqués are a good place to introduce a contrasting motif. It was machine quilted with computerized *marumon* (circular motifs), and an all-over pattern specially designed to resemble *sakiori's* coloured warp threads. The scrap quilt version overleaf is hand quilted in big stitch, with traditional family crests used for the circles.

Long-arm quilter and all-over quilting pattern design: Leslie Carol Taylor of North Sea Quilters (see Suppliers)
Circular motif quilting design: Dawn Cheetham

Kamon Quilt

For this quilt, the large scale *kamon* (Japanese family crest) print was perfect for featuring in the circles, so I reduced the circle size to fit the motif. Most of the 1½in (3.8cm) wide strips were cut from fat quarters, so only two blocks could be cut from each set of eight strips. Many fabrics have a faux patchwork print, which can give a complex effect. Ample indigo blues tone down the touches of brighter colours for a more antique look.

The construction of this quilt is identical to the brightly coloured version. Simple big stitch hand quilting along every fourth strip imitates the appearance of plain sashiko on old fabrics. Rather than mark the stitching lines, a piece of masking tape was used to guide the stitching, which was peeled off and repositioned for the next quilting line.

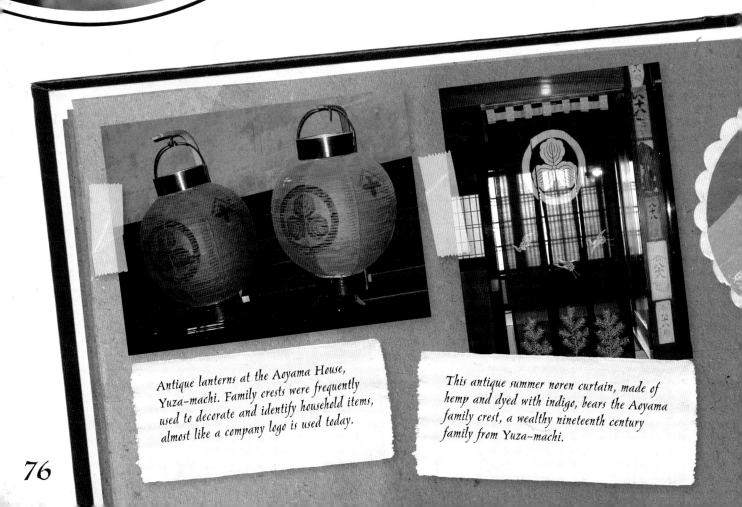

Antique lanterns at the Aoyama House, Yuza-machi. Family crests were frequently used to decorate and identify household items, almost like a company logo is used today.

This antique summer noren curtain, made of hemp and dyed with indigo, bears the Aoyama family crest, a wealthy nineteenth century family from Yuza-machi.

Kimono

Japanese Robes

The kimono outline is an instantly recognisable Japanese design. This quilt motif is shaped like a real kimono, displayed from the back, with the front panels held open – the way that kimono *karinui* (untailored fabric) are usually displayed in shops. Seasonal flowers are popular themes and this quilt has a different kimono for every month.

The 12in (30.5cm) kimono blocks are made using freezer paper appliqué, which also allows the fabric to be shown as a continuous piece, imitating the *tsukesage* style of kimono dyeing, where patterns flow across seams. Using the same background fabric for each block unifies the design. It was free-hand quilted on a long-arm machine, with an added a design of clamshells in the border and feathers along the shaded sashing to balance the rich fabrics.

Many styles of kimono are displayed as tacked (basted) fabrics, which customers can have tailored to fit. Brighter colours and larger motifs are associated with young women's kimono styles, like the long-sleeved furisode.

Fabric Focus

The fabrics used in this quilt were all from the same manufacturer, who brought out a 'flowers of the month' series, but you can theme your kimono around any patterns or motifs. Wearing seasonal flowers, foliage and other motifs on kimono has been developed over centuries and Japanese people associate some plants with very specific times of year. A chart overleaf explains the motifs in these fabrics. A fat quarter of each allows you to select the part of the print you want to use.

Kimono Quilt

You will need

- Twelve fat quarters for kimono fabrics – see box below

- Twelve 12½in (31.8cm) squares of background fabric

- Twelve assorted block borders for each block:
  two strips 12½in x 1½in (31.8cm x 3.8cm)
  two strips 14½in x 1½in (36.8cm x 3.8cm)

- Shaded cotton for sashing 41in (104cm) – see Tip opposite

- Fabric for border:
  two strips 66½in x 7½in (168.9cm x 19cm)
  two strips 64½in x 7½in (163.8cm x 19cm)

- Twelve 12½in (31.8cm) squares of freezer paper (the roll type is wide enough)

- Sewing thread to tone with patchwork

- Quilting thread to contrast with patchwork (if machine quilting)

- Backing fabric to coordinate with patchwork – see Wadding and Backing

- Wadding (batting) – see Wadding and Backing

- Binding fabric 300in (762cm) length

Finished quilt: 80in x 64in (203.2 x 162.6cm)

Kimono Fabrics

Each appliqué kimono only uses one 12½in (31.7cm) fabric square, but you can be selective about which part of the fabric you use if you have a larger piece. I used flower-themed prints for the kimono.

January – pine
February – plum
March – narcissus
April – cherry blossom
May – wisteria
June – iris
July – peony
August – morning glory
September – Chinese bellflower
October – chrysanthemum
November – maple
December – camellia

Making the Appliqués

1 Following the measurements in Fig 1 below, draft a master template for the kimono block or photocopy, which I found to be the easiest way. Alternatively, enlarge the pattern given here by 200%. Trace twelve kimono shapes on to the freezer paper and cut out carefully.

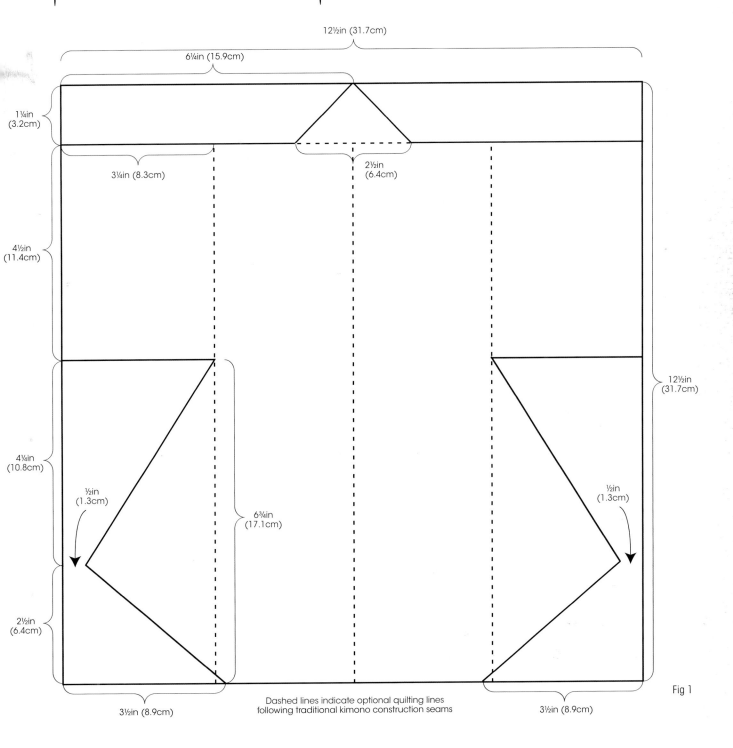

12½in (31.7cm)

6¼in (15.9cm)

1¼in (3.2cm)

3¼in (8.3cm)

2½in (6.4cm)

4½in (11.4cm)

12½in (31.7cm)

4¼in (10.8cm)

½in (1.3cm)

6¾in (17.1cm)

½in (1.3cm)

2½in (6.4cm)

3½in (8.9cm)

Dashed lines indicate optional quilting lines following traditional kimono construction seams

3½in (8.9cm)

Fig 1

2 For each kimono block appliqué, use the iron on a cool setting to iron the freezer paper template on to the back of each piece of kimono fabric, selecting the area you wish to feature for the kimono. Cut out the kimono, cutting a generous ¼in (6mm) away from the edge of the paper to allow for the appliqué hem, as shown in Fig 2, except for at the ends of the sleeves and the bottom hem, where a seam allowance is already included – this will be sewn into the patchwork seam later. Clip the seam allowance at the points indicated by the arrows. Press the hem allowance over the edge of the freezer paper shapes with the iron on a slightly higher temperature, but being careful not to scorch your fabrics and only pressing the very edge. Allow the pieces to cool.

3 Pin a kimono to a centre backing square, so the freezer paper is sandwiched between the appliqué and the backing square, lining up the sleeve and hem edges with the square, with raw edges all tucked under, arranging pins as in Fig 3. Add more pins to hold the appliqué securely in place. The appliqué can be hand or machine sewn in place – see Appliqué. Turn each block over and cut away the background fabric, leaving a generous ¼in (6mm) allowance behind each kimono. Remove the paper by peeling it away from the back of the kimono. Scrunching up the paper along the edges will help loosen it from the appliqué stitches. Appliqué kimono to all twelve blocks.

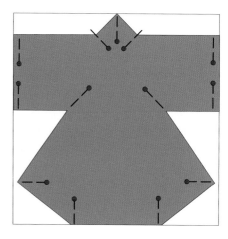

Fig 3

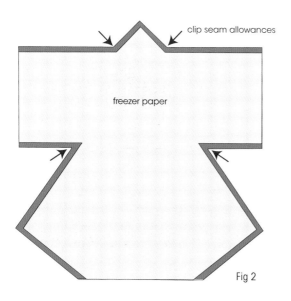

clip seam allowances

freezer paper

Fig 2

Sewing the Block Borders

4 Machine sew two 12½in x 1½in (21.8 x 3.8cm) border strips to the top and bottom of each appliqué block. Sew the two 14½in x 1½in (36.8cm x 3.8cm) strips to the block sides, as in Fig 4. Press seams towards the outside of the block each time.

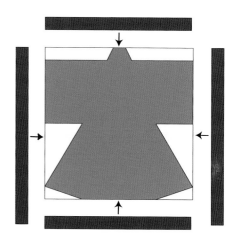

Fig 4

Trusted Tip…

Real kimono often feature more of the design motifs on the 'skirt' and upper body, as the centre of the kimono are covered by the obi sash when worn. You do not have to be realistic with your appliqués – just use the kimono shape to frame your favourite part of the fabric print.

Fig 6

Cutting the Sashing Strips

5 Shaded fabric gives a woven appearance to the sashing.
Some shaded fabrics shade symmetrically from edge to centre
and back again, others from side to side. For either shading, cut
sixteen 2½in (6.4cm) wide strips across the fabric width first, as
in Fig 5, and then cut eleven 30½in (77.5cm) long sashing strips
from the strip centres and nine 16½in (41.9cm) sashing strips
from either end.

7 Start assembling the quilt top using a part-sewn seam method
– see Sewing a Part-Sewn Seam. Machine sew the sashing to the
blocks, starting with the seams indicated by the blue lines in Fig
7, sewing only about 2in (5cm) of each seam. Continue joining the
blocks and sashing along the seams indicated by the yellow lines,
also sewing only about 2in (5cm) until all the blocks and sashing
strips are joined at the beginning and end of each strip. Finger press
seam allowances towards the sashing strips. Working your way
across the patchwork, return to each partly sewn seam and complete
sewing the centre section of each seam, overlapping the previous
stitches by about ½in (1.3cm). Press seams towards the sashing.

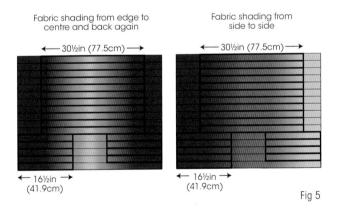

Fabric shading from edge to
centre and back again

← 30½in (77.5cm) →

← 16½in →
(41.9cm)

Fabric shading from
side to side

← 30½in (77.5cm) →

← 16½in →
(41.9cm)

Fig 5

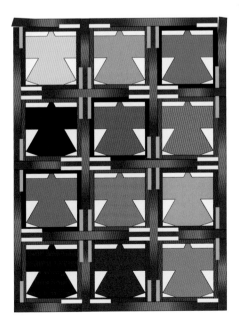

Fig 7

Assembling the Quilt Top

6 Lay out the blocks as in Fig 6. The blocks were arranged
in the same order that the motifs are used through the year,
starting with pine for January in the top right corner, but arrange
your blocks as you wish, balancing the fabrics across the quilt.
Position the sashing strips in the correct places, turning the strips
around to obtain the shading effect.

Quilting and Finishing

9 This quilt was free-hand quilted on a long-arm machine, with each kimono block treated individually. A pebble design pushes down the block backgrounds, allowing the kimono fabrics to be the main focus. The woven effect created with the shaded sashing fabric was emphasized by quilting along each strip. The border waves print suggested a clamshell pattern. The little kimono also lend themselves to being quilted to imitate real life kimono seams, with vertical lines up the centre back and down from each shoulder, as indicated by the dashed lines in Fig 1, which could be done with a walking foot on a domestic sewing machine or be hand quilted.

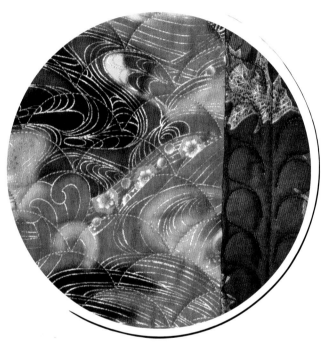

Adding the Border

8 Measure your quilt top and cut fabric strips for the borders – see Adding a Border. Sew the 66½in x 7½in (168.9cm x 19cm) long quilt borders to either side first, and then add the shorter border strips across the top and bottom. Press seams towards the quilt border. Layer and tack (baste) the quilt ready for quilting, if quilting by hand or domestic machine – see Making a Quilt Sandwich.

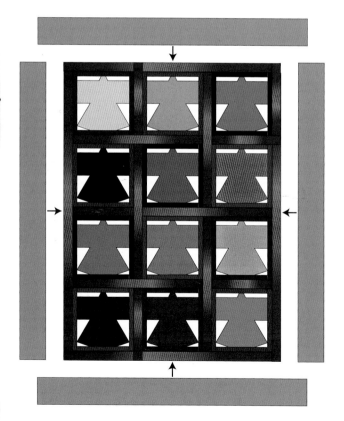

Fig 7

10 Bind your quilt to finish – see Binding. Select a binding fabric to coordinate with your quilt, such as the dark blue used here. Although there is a lot of black in some of the kimono prints, this could have looked too stark for the binding and the blue is a little softer. There's no need to match the border colour exactly and a slightly darker binding will help to frame the quilt.

The fabrics for the kimono were the starting point for this quilt. As they included many colours and values, a neutral background worked best. The free-hand machine quilting was kept simple and classic for the kimono but the background was quilted in a pebble design, so the kimono appear more three-dimensional. The threads were coordinated to the fabrics in the sashing strips and border, allowing the kimono fabrics to take centre stage.

Long-arm quilter: Karen Florey at the Running Chicken (see Suppliers)

Hanui
Patchwork Kimono

Until early in the twentieth century kimono were often worn as a layered set, with the inner *dounuki* kimono sometimes made of patchwork, with the hem and cuffs coordinating with the outer kimono. The fashion survives in the *hanui* kimono worn on the last night of the *Nishimonai* summer festival in Ugo-machi, Akita Prefecture. These *hanui* are made from scraps of precious cloth, including valuable antique silks.

The *hanui* motif makes a splendid quilt centre, and here a printed Japanese-style quilt panel is the main focus. The sleeves are a patchwork of scraps and the checked background gives a homely feeling. A mitred outer border creates a picture-frame effect around the quilt, simply hand quilted with big stitch accents on the kimono, in a faux sashiko style.

Kimono fabrics are displayed for sale with the skirt sections spread out to show off the designs. The patterns on formal kimono are dyed to form a continuous pattern when the panels are sewn together in the correct order.

Multicoloured koi create flashes of colour in the deep pool at Teien, a private garden near Yuza-machi.

Fabric Focus

Panels with Japanese designs are a regular feature of quilt fabric collections and make a stunning focus to a quilt. Select the other fabrics in coordinating colours but make sure the background fabric is a good contrast so the kimono shape stands out. If the panel is a slightly different size, add extra strips and borders to fit the back of the 'kimono'. The border print was from the same range as the koi panel and the mitred corners show off the broad stripes in the design.

Hanui Quilt

You will need

- One feature panel trimmed to 43½in x 20½in (110.5cm x 52.1cm)

- Border fabric for feature panel two strips 43½in x 2½in (110.5cm x 6.4cm)

- Fabric for centre background – see step 1 for pieces

- Print fabric for kimono – see step 1

- Assorted prints for kimono sleeves in matched pairs – see step 1

- For the inner border:
  two strips 48½in x 1½in (123.2cm x 3.8cm)
  two strips 5½in x 1½in (14cm x 3.8cm)

- For the outer border:
  two strips 73in x 8in (185.4 x 20.3cm)
  two strips 67in x 8in (170.2 x 20.3cm)

- Sewing thread to tone with patchwork

- Quilting thread to tone with patchwork (if hand quilting)

- Perle no. 12 or similar thread for big stitch quilting

- Backing fabric to coordinate with patchwork – see Wadding and Backing

- Wadding (batting) – see Wadding and Backing

- Binding fabric 300in (762cm) length

Finished quilt: 72in x 66in (182.9 x 167.6cm) approximately

Cutting the Fabric Pieces

1 From the fabric for the centre background cut the following:
two pieces each 34½in x 12½in (87.6cm x 31.8cm),
two strips 24¼in x 2½in (61.6cm x 6.4cm).
From the print fabric for the kimono cut the following:
one piece 9½in x 24½in (24.1 x 62.2cm) for back hem panel,
two pieces 32in x 11in (81.3 x 27.9cm) for front panels,
two strips 5½in x 2½in (14 x 6.4cm) for collar ends,
one strip 2½in x 5in (6.4cm x 12.7cm) for collar top.
From the assorted prints for the kimono sleeves cut the following:
A – two strips 10½in x 2½in (26.7cm x 6.4cm),
B – two strips 8½in x 2½in (21.6cm x 6.4cm),
C – two strips 8½in x 2½in (21.6cm x 6.4cm) (different fabric),
D – two strips 14½in x 4½in (36.8cm x 11.4cm),
E – two squares 4½in (11.4cm),
F – two strips 8½in x 6½in (21.6cm x 16.5cm),
G – two strips 6½in x 2½in (16.5cm x 6.4cm),
H – two strips 8½in x 4½in (21.6cm x 11.4cm).

Sewing the Patchwork

2 Using ¼in (6mm) seams throughout, machine sew the two 43½in x 2½in (110.5cm x 6.4cm) border strips to either side of the centre back panel, as shown in Fig 1. Press towards the strips. Machine sew the 9½in x 24½in (24.1cm x 62.2cm) piece across the bottom edge. Press towards the bottom edge.

4 Arrange the 2½in x 5in (6.4cm x 12.7cm) collar top strip and the two 24¼in x 2½in (61.6cm x 6.4cm) background strips right sides together as in Fig 3. Machine sew along the dashed black lines and trim off the excess fabric by cutting away the triangles as shown by the solid blue lines, leaving a ¼in (6mm) seam allowance. Press the seams towards the collar top triangle.

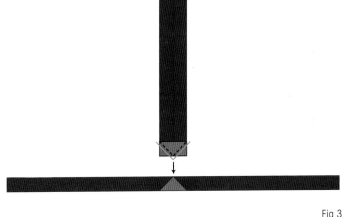

Fig 3

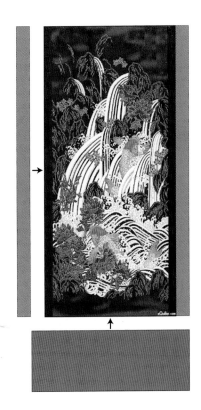

Fig 1

Making the Appliqué

5 Following the dimensions in Fig 4, cut the two 32in x 11in (81.3cm x 27.9cm) pieces to make the front kimono panels.

3 Arrange and machine sew the patchwork panels for the kimono sleeves, as in Fig 2. Press seams downwards and towards the outer edges.

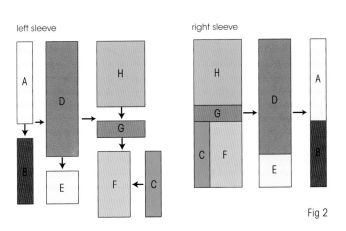

Fig 2

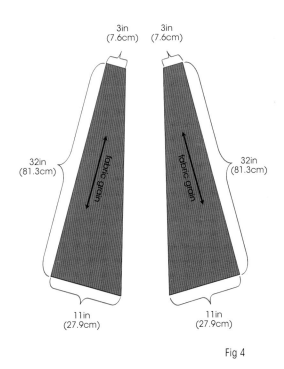

Fig 4

6 Fold and press a ¼in (6mm) hem across the bottom of each of the 5½in x 2½in (14cm x 6.4cm) strips for the collar ends. Fold and press the same hem on the long right side of one strip to make the collar end for the left side of the kimono, and the hem on the left side of the strip to make the right side collar end. Pin and machine sew one collar end to each front kimono panel, as shown in Fig 5, positioning the collar strip about ¼in (6mm) from the end of the kimono panel.

Fig 5

7 Fold and press under a ¼in (6mm) hem along the two straight edges of each front kimono panel, pressing the seam allowance from step 5 under the edge of the front panel too. Position and pin one front panel to one 34½in x 12½in (87.6cm x 31.8cm) background piece, as shown in Fig 6. Hand or machine appliqué to the background panel – see Appliqué, sewing along all the appliqué panel edges except those lining up with the background panel edges. Trim the excess appliqué fabric to match the background panel across each panel top. Turn the panel over and trim away the background fabric behind the kimono front panel, leaving a generous ¼in (6mm) seam allowance inside the appliqué.

Fig 6

Making the Quilt Centre

8 Using Fig 7 as a guide, arrange and machine sew the quilt centre. Sew the sleeves to the appliqué panels and press seams towards the kimono sleeves. Sew these panels to either side of the kimono centre panel and press seams towards the centre panel. Sew the collar section from step 3 across the top of the kimono and press seams towards the kimono.

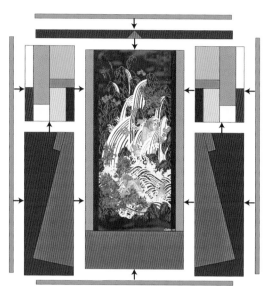

Fig 7

Adding the Mitred Border

9 Using the two 73in x 8in (185.4cm x 20.3cm) and two 67in x 8in (170.2cm x 20.3cm) border strips, sew the outer border to the quilt (Fig 8). With reference to Fig 9A and B, sew one border strip at a time, lining up the centre of the strip with the quilt centre.

Fig 8

Pin and sew the central 52½in (133.3cm) section of the side strips and 50½in (128.3cm) of the top and bottom to the quilt centre, starting and finishing ¼in (6mm) from the end of the quilt centre each time, with a few backstitches (the sewing line is shown in blue for clarity).

10 Fold down and press the top of the left corner strip on a 45 degree angle, as shown in Fig 10. Fold and press the adjacent corner strip to match the mitre. With right sides together, align the fold lines on the two strips, pin and sew along the fold to make the mitre, back stitching at either end. Repeat with the other corners. There will be two triangles of fabric left at the ends of the border strips, so trim the mitred seam allowance to ¼in (6mm) to remove these. Press the mitred seams to one side and then press the long border seams towards the quilt centre.

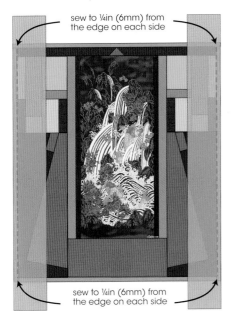

sew to ¼in (6mm) from the edge on each side

sew to ¼in (6mm) from the edge on each side

Fig 9A

back view

Fig 10

flip the sewn side borders open, out of the way so the top and bottom borders can be sewn

Fig 9B

Trusted Tip...

Borders with straight rather than mitred corners could be used if preferred – see Adding a Border. A mitred border shows off the striped print to great advantage but the corner effect would be wasted on a fabric without a strong sense of direction in the print. A square border is also more economical on fabric than a mitre, which leaves waste triangles when the mitred seams are trimmed.

Quilting and Finishing

11 Layer and tack (baste) the quilt ready for quilting, if quilting by hand or domestic machine – see Making a Quilt Sandwich. Hand quilting in the ditch secured the quilt layers before extra quilting was added following lines in the koi panel. Stitch a line down the centre back of the kimono panel, to imitate the seam normally found here. Blank areas at the top and bottom of the panel had additional horizontal lines added in big stitch, suggesting mist, and big stitch was added to the kimono sleeve seams, about ⅜in (1cm) from each seam line. Lines in the kimono hem fabric, background weave and border stripe were simple to hand quilt. The floral border strip was big stitch quilted with a simple interlocking zigzag along its length, as the flowers and leaves were too complex to hand quilt easily.

12 Bind your quilt to finish – see Binding. Select a binding fabric to coordinate with your quilt, such as the black used here, which gives the effect of a lacquer frame.

Trusted Tip...

Any quilt where a picture panel is the main focus needs to be quilted with sensitivity to the overall design of the image. Use lines and motifs in the panel as your starting point rather than imposing an unrelated pattern all over the quilt. It is not necessary to quilt every line or motif in a design – stitch along lines that will add some dimension to the design and resist the temptation to quilt too much and flatten the panel.

The rich, warm colours in the panel are echoed by the border and coordinating fabrics. Elements in the panel were emphasized by hand quilting along lines in the design. Elsewhere, there is hand quilting in the ditch and along lines in the orange diamond print and the background fabric. Big stitch quilting is added to the edges of the patchwork pieces in the sleeves, imitating the topstitching seen on real *hanui*, and in simple lines as a filler in the top and bottom of the koi panel. For domestic machine quilting try a similar combination, with free-motion quilting around floral details.

Pattern
Inspirations

This section contains attractive projects that feature some of the blocks used in the quilts, including a handy storage bag, a comfortable floor cushion, a stylish table runner and a useful tote. Making these projects will allow you to practise the techniques needed to create the quilts and make something useful at the same time. If you use the same fabrics and colours as the quilts they will coordinate beautifully. The projects can also use up any orphan or leftover blocks you may have from past projects, with advice given on adapting the designs.

Komebukuro
Rice Bag

You will find many uses for this drawstring bag, which is in the style of a traditional *komebukuro* (rice bag). It would make a great store for a fabric stash, a scarf collection or anything you like. Make it with any set of five square blocks – perhaps some left over from a quilt. The five lining panels can be different fabrics. The size of the finished block determines the bag size.

The bag shown far right uses *irori* blocks in the same fabrics as the Irori Quilt. The blocks were machine quilted using the big stitch quilting pattern from the quilt, with an extra curved line to create a four-petalled motif in the block centre, and an additional line of contour quilting.

The second bag (right) uses *igeta* blocks in black and pink fabrics from the Igeta Quilt, which were machine quilted in the ditch around the *igeta* shape, with extra quilting in cream for a sashiko effect. Strip-pieced panels, like the Furoshiki Quilt borders or the strip blocks in the Sakiori Quilt, are the kind of patchwork traditionally used for *komebukuro* bags.

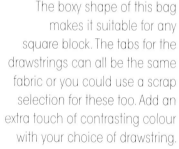

The boxy shape of this bag makes it suitable for any square block. The tabs for the drawstrings can all be the same fabric or you could use a scrap selection for these too. Add an extra touch of contrasting colour with your choice of drawstring.

Fabric Focus

Sewing a few extra blocks can be useful when arranging an asymmetric quilt, such as the Irori Quilt, and they can always be used up on a smaller project. Alternatively, use the fewer blocks needed for the bag to try out fabric combinations.

Storage Bag

You will need

- Five square quilt blocks
- Five squares of lining fabric the same size as the quilt blocks
- Five squares of wadding (batting) slightly larger than the quilt blocks
- Five squares of backing fabric slightly larger than the quilt blocks
- Two pieces of cord for drawstrings each four times longer than the block size
- Twelve 4in x 3in (10.2cm x 7.6cm) strips of patchwork fabric for bag loops
- Sewing and quilting threads to tone with fabrics

Finished size: 9in (23cm) cube approximately

Making the Bag Lining panels

1 Arrange the squares of lining fabric to form a cross shape, as shown in Fig 1A. The block in the middle is the base of the bag lining. Sew one square on either side of the base square, starting and finishing each seam ¼in (6mm) from the edge of the patchwork, with a few backstitches. Join the two remaining blocks to form the cross shape, starting and finishing each seam the same way (Fig 1B).

2 Now join the corners of the cross to form a cube, but leave a 5in (12.7cm) long gap unsewn in the middle of the last seam (the bag will be turned right side out through this gap, so don't make it any smaller). Press side seams to one side.

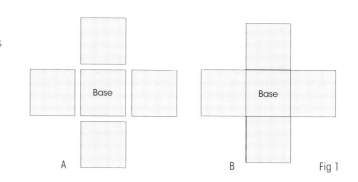

A   B   Fig 1

Making the Drawstring Loops

3 Fold each 4in x 3in (10.2cm x 7.6cm) strip in half lengthwise and press, as shown in Fig 2. Open out the fabric and fold the sides of the fabric to meet the crease running down the middle and press again to make a strip with four layers of fabric folded into it. Stitch along each long edge, sewing close to the edge. Leave the ends raw (these will be encased in the top of the bag).

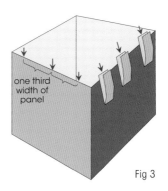

Fig 3

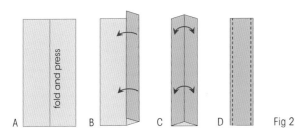

A   B   C   D   Fig 2

7 Turn the bag lining inside out. Place the bag outer inside the bag lining, lining up the corners of the cube shape formed by the bag and the top edges of bag and lining. Sew the bag to the lining, sewing all around the top of the bag.

Making the Bag Panels

4 Take your five patchwork squares and layer each with wadding (batting) and backing as described in Making a Quilt Sandwich, checking that the patchwork is square and not distorted (use a square ruler to help you, or check the diagonal measurements are the same). Quilt as desired. I used the big stitch quilting pattern from step 8 of the Tatami Stripes Quilt as a starting point, but adding an extra curved line to the pattern to create a four petal motif in the block centre. An extra line of contour quilting was also added. Machine sew around each completed panel. Trim the wadding and backing to the edge of the panel and overlock or zigzag the edges all round.

5 Sew the bag panels and base together as for the lining in steps 1 and 2, but without the gap in the final seam. Press side seams to one side.

Assembling the Bag

6 Fold each drawstring loop in half, bringing the two raw ends together, and pin to the outside edge of the top of the outer bag panel with the fold pointing downwards, so the raw ends are standing up ¼in (6mm) above the top edge of the bag, as shown in Fig 3. Arrange the loops at equal distances around the bag, three per panel, with the central loop matching up to the middle of the block. Pin each loop securely or tack (baste) in place.

8 Place your hand through the opening left in the lining side seam and turn the whole bag right side out through this gap. Press the seam around the bag edge, being careful not to squash the wadding. The drawstring loops will be standing up around the top of the bag. Topstitch around the top of the bag, ⅛in (3mm) from the edge. Close up the gap in the side of the lining by slipstitching or ladder stitching the fabrics together by hand.

9 Thread each drawstring through the drawstring loops, taking care not to twist the drawstrings around each other. Knot the ends of each drawstring together to make a loop and fluff out the ends of the cord to finish.

Zabuton *Floor Cushion*

Floor cushions called *zabuton* are a feature of traditional Japanese interiors, beginning as straw mat cushions used by the nobility about a thousand years ago. Reflecting the idea that guests of honour are still given a cushion to sit on, a larger cushion makes an attractive focus for a special chair or can be used, Japanese style, for extra seating on the floor. Traditional *zabuton* are approximately 20in–22in (50.8cm–55.9cm), slightly rectangular and flatter than western cushions, but the cushion shown here will fit a square cushion pad. Finish the cushion with either a zipped closure or an envelope back (instructions are given for both).

A single block from the Shimacho Quilt is 24in (61cm) square and is ideal for a cushion front. I used matching fabrics, so the two projects can be used together. Other square blocks could also be used – see overleaf.

With just one block, each patchwork print was used only once, although they are repeated in the Shimacho Quilt so the cushion coordinates well. The smaller cushion panel was easy to turn around while machine quilting, enabling a walking foot to be used to stitch around each fabric sample, which contrasts with the free-motion quilting used on the main quilt.

Fabric Focus

A matching cushion makes a good project to use up any fabrics left over from one of the larger quilts or to experiment with a colour scheme before committing yourself to making something bigger. It can also provide a useful panel to try out a quilting design which may or may not be used for the main quilt.

Floor Cushion

You will need

- One patchwork panel for cushion front (see step 1)

- Plain calico (muslin) for backing, larger than the patchwork

- Wadding (batting), larger than the patchwork

- One piece of fabric for cushion back, the same size as the quilted and trimmed cushion front plus one zipper with closed end, about 2in (5cm) shorter than cushion side **or** two pieces of fabric for an envelope back (see Tip below)

- Sewing thread to tone with patchwork

- Quilting thread to tone with patchwork (if machine quilting)

- Three flat buttons if using an envelope back (optional)

- Cushion pad to fit cover

Finished size: 24in (61cm) square

Trusted Tip...

For an envelope back the two backing panels must overlap enough to avoid the back gaping when in use, but not so much that it is difficult to insert the pad. Cut each panel the same length as the side of the finished cushion panel, but only three-fifths of the width. For example, suitable back panels for a 24in (61cm) square finished cushion would be 24½in x 14½in (62.2cm x 36.8cm).

Cutting the Fabrics

1 To make one Shimacho block as shown in Fig 1, cut the following from assorted feature fabrics:

A – six 2½in (6.4cm) squares,

B – two 4½in (11.4cm) squares,

C – one 6½in (16.5cm) square,

D – three 4½in x 2½in (11.4cm x 6.4cm) strips,

E – two 6½in x 4½in (16.5cm x 11.4cm) strips,

F – one 10½in x 6½in (26.7cm x 16.5cm) strip,

G – one 8½in x 6½in (21.6cm x 16.5cm) strip.

Using Other Blocks

Other square blocks may be used or combined to make a cushion front or have extra borders added to increase their size. For example, four 8in (20.3cm) fan blocks from the Sensu Quilt would make a smaller 16in (40.6cm) cushion. One of the 14in (35.6cm) square blocks in the Masu Quilt can be increased to 18in (45.7cm) by adding another square border of 2½in (6.4cm) wide strips. A single 12in (30.5cm) block from the Kimono Quilt can be made into a bigger cushion panel with a wide border all round. Smaller Japanese motif quilt panels, about the size of a fat quarter, would make beautiful larger *zabuton* cushions by adding a narrower version of the border on the Furoshiki Quilt.

You will also need border fabric 14in x 43in–44in (35.6cm x 109.2cm–111.8cm). Cut this into nine 1½in (3.8cm) strips across the width of the fabric. Sub-cut the following strips: two 11½in (29.2cm); two 9½in (24.1cm); twelve 7½in (19cm); eighteen 5½in (14cm) and thirty 3½in (8.9cm).

Making the Block

2 Follow steps 4–7 for the Shimacho Quilt to make one block, as shown in Fig 1.

Quilting the Cushion Panel

3 Layer and tack (baste) the cushion panel ready for quilting, if quilting by hand or domestic machine – see Making A Quilt Sandwich. Quilt the patchwork pieces in the ditch around the seam lines and add a few extra meandering lines of quilting in the larger pieces. The borders can be quilted with a decorative stitch or left unquilted. The cushion can be finished with a zip closure or an envelope back. Trim the sandwich and then zigzag or overlock the edges of the panel before assembling the cushion. Decide which method you prefer and use the relevant instructions that follow.

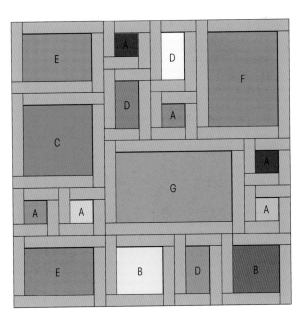

Fig 1

Assembling with a Zip Closure

4 Place the patchwork and cushion backing panel right sides together. Use ½in (1.3cm) seams throughout assembly. With right sides together, machine or hand tack (baste) across the bottom edge (see dashed red line in Fig 2). Machine sew 1in (2.5cm) at the beginning and end of the tacking, starting and finishing with a few backstitches, as shown by the blue line.

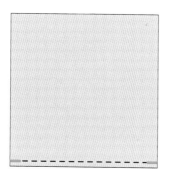

Fig 2

5 Press the seam open. From the wrong side, tack the zip in place (make sure the zip pull is facing the right way to open your cushion from the outside!). With the zip foot on the sewing machine, sew the zip in place (see dashed black lines in Fig 3). Check the zip opens properly and remove tacking (basting).

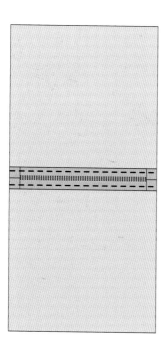

Fig 3

6 With the zip open, place the other three edges of the panel and backing together, pin, and machine sew all round with a ½in (1.3cm) seam allowance. Clip corners, turn right side out through the zip opening, press the seam and insert the pad.

Assembling with an Envelope Back

7 Hem one long edge of each cushion backing panel by turning over a doubled ¼in (6mm) hem and zigzag or overlock the other edges. Place the patchwork and one of the backing pieces right sides together and pin, as shown in Fig 4.

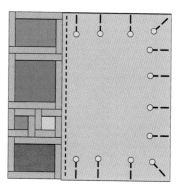

Fig 4

8 Place the second backing piece right sides together, overlapping the first piece, and pin. Machine sew around the edge, with a ½in (1.3cm) seam allowance, as shown by the dashed line in Fig 5. Clip the corners and turn right sides out. Insert the cushion pad through the gap.

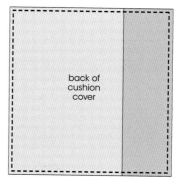

back of cushion cover

Fig 5

Trusted Tip...

On the envelope back, if the panel overlap will be less than 2in (5cm), add an optional button fastening to the panel edges, working the buttonholes (by hand or machine) on the first backing panel before sewing the panels in place and adding the buttons when the cushion cover is complete. Choose flat buttons so they don't catch so easily on furniture or carpets.

Ranna *Table Runner*

A table runner makes an attractive feature whether your table is a low one like a Japanese *kotatsu* or a Western dining table. The runner can coordinate with many styles of tableware – blue and white porcelain, rustic stoneware or colourfully glazed pottery. Japanese ceramics are still produced regionally and the fabrics used here reflect the earthy glazes of the Hirashimizu pottery near Yamagata, as well as patterns from blue and white china.

Each end of the runner has a single 12in (30.5cm) appliqué block from the Kimono Quilt, made from *yukata* cottons. These are bordered with strips, so the finished blocks are 14in (35.6cm) wide. The centre of the runner has strip sections and narrower strips could also be included if desired. The kimono are quilted to indicate the garments' seam lines. Simple machine quilting across the strips with different thread colours produces an effect like *sakiori* rag weaving – see the Sakiori Quilt. The backing is bagged out, so no binding is needed.

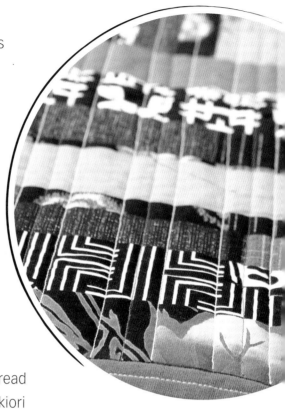

Simple Seminole strip construction means that making the runner longer or shorter is very easy – simply add more strips to the central section. Make it to fit the length of your table or to hang over the ends, whichever you prefer.

Fabric Focus

Use up left-over strips to make the central strip-pieced section of this runner. Light and dark fabrics are alternated in the strips along the length to avoid having predominantly light or dark areas. Woven checks and stripes can be mixed with prints for a homely effect. The kimono blocks give a bigger area that can be used to showcase two large-scale prints.

Table Runner

You will need

- Two patchwork panels for runner ends (see step 1)
- Seven assorted 2½in (6.4cm) wide strips for the central sections (see step 3)
- Sewing thread to tone with patchwork
- Quilting threads to tone and contrast with patchwork
- Wadding (batting), larger than the patchwork
- One piece of fabric for runner backing, same size as runner panel (see step 4)

Finished size: 14in x 68in
(35.6cm x 172.7cm)

Using Other Blocks

Two patchwork blocks from the Kimono Quilt were used to make this runner, but other blocks could be used. A narrower or shorter table runner can easily be adapted by changing the blocks used at the ends and adjusting the width to suit. For example, the 10in (25.4cm) block from the Kunimoto Quilt could be used for a 10in (25.4cm) wide runner or the 8in (20.3cm) block from the Sensu Quilt for an 8in (20.3cm) wide piece.

Cutting the Fabrics

1 To make two kimono blocks with borders as shown in Fig 1, cut the following pieces of fabric:
two fat quarters or 12½in (31.8cm) squares for kimono fabrics and two 12½in (31.8cm) squares of background fabric.

You will also need two assorted block borders, so for each block cut the following pieces of fabric:
two 12½in x 1½in (31.8 x 3.8cm) strips and
two 14½in x 1½in (36.8cm x 3.8cm) strips.

Making the Block

2 To make two bordered kimono blocks follow the instructions in steps 1–4 for the Kimono Quilt.

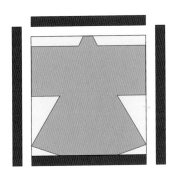

Fig 1

Sewing the Strip Patchwork

3 The 2½in (6.3cm) wide strips can be seven strips across the full width of the fabric 42in–44in (106.7cm–111.8cm) or fourteen 14½in (36.8cm) and seven 12½in (31.8cm) strips. To make the strip patchwork sections with seven full-width strips, machine sew pairs of strips together using ¼in (6mm) seams throughout. Sew pairs together until all seven are sewn. Press each piece of patchwork so all the seams lie in the same direction. Cut two 14½in (36.8cm) wide sections from the patchwork, lining up with the opposite end from the selvedges for your first cut, as shown by the red lines in Fig 2. Cut one 12½in (31.8cm) section from the remaining patchwork.

Alternatively, make two patchwork sections from seven 14½in (36.8cm) strips and one section, for the centre of the runner, from seven 12½in (31.8cm) strips.

Assembling the Patchwork

4 Machine sew the strip sections and the kimono blocks together to make the table runner panel, as shown in Fig 3. Once sewn together and pressed use the panel as a pattern to cut out a piece of backing fabric the same size.

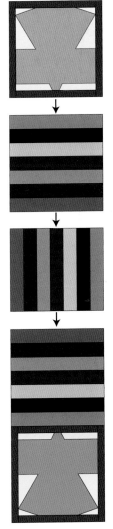

Fig 3

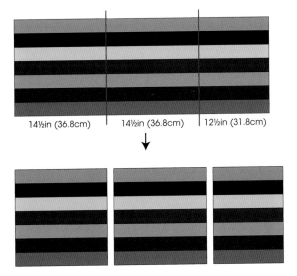

14½in (36.8cm)   14½in (36.8cm)   12½in (31.8cm)

Fig 2

Backing and Quilting

5 Tack (baste) the wadding (batting) to the wrong side of the backing fabric, as if making a quilt sandwich with only two layers, spreading the wadding out and laying the backing right side up on to it. Tack with stitches rather than pins, which tend to catch on each other when turning the runner right side out (Fig 4). Lay the patchwork panel on top over the backing and wadding sandwich, right sides together with the backing, and smooth it out. Pin and machine sew all around using a ¼in (6mm) seam allowance, and leaving a 4in (10.2cm) gap unsewn at one end of the runner. The whole runner will be turned right side out through this gap, so don't make it too small.

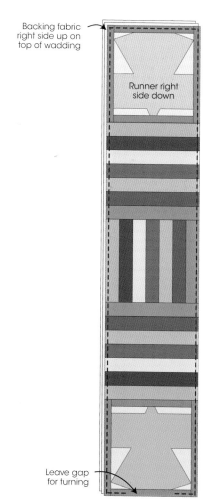

Backing fabric right side up on top of wadding

Runner right side down

Leave gap for turning

Fig 4

6 Trim the backing to the same size as the runner. Trim the excess wadding from the seam allowance and across the gap. Clip little triangles off across the corners to reduce bulk, cutting about ⅛in (3mm) away from the stitches, and 'bag out', turning the runner right side out through the unsewn gap. Smooth the top over the wadding and backing, tack the layers together before quilting and slipstitch the gap closed when complete.

7 Hand sewing around the edge creates a crisp finish. Work from the back, taking a short running stitch through the backing and a longer running stitch through the seam allowance inside the edge, about ⅛in (3mm) from the edge. Don't let the stitching show on the front.

8 Quilt simple lines across the strip patchwork. Quilt the kimono along where the kimono seam lines would be (down the centre back and from shoulder to hem on each side, as shown by the dashed lines on Fig 1 of the Kimono Quilt) and around the kimono and the block border. The runner shown is machine quilted using a walking foot but hand quilt if you prefer.

Trusted Tip...

If hand quilting, a simple line of big stitch quilting down the centre of each strip in cream or beige thread would create a sashiko-style accent.

Kaban *Bag*

This simple bag or *kaban*, which is fully lined, is an everyday necessity for carrying shopping, books or your current stitching project. Two square blocks form the main part of each side of the bag, which has a simple boxed base and cloth handles. Extra fabric strips are added at the top and bottom of each panel, so the bag is really two rectangles joined by the strip at the base.

Two 14in (35.6cm) blocks, as used in the Masu Quilt are used for the side panels. Two Kimono blocks with borders would be the same size, or a smaller version could be made using two Kunimoto or Sensu blocks. The outer bag panel is used as a pattern to cut out the lining, so resizing the bag is very easy. The patchwork is quilted in the ditch and around the masu 'boxes', helping to give the bag shape. For a very thin, lightweight bag, quilt the blocks on to an interlining but omit the wadding (batting).

Two blocks and some simple extra piecing make this bag quick to create – ideal for a sophisticated gift bag. Keep the quilting simple and use the walking foot on your machine. Use heavier fabric, like denim or canvas furnishing for the base and leave unquilted.

Fabric Focus

Change the style of your bag with different fabric combinations – colourful gold prints are used here but the bag would have a different mood made in tranquil taupe, cool blue and white *yukata* cottons or with rustic blues, creams and browns. The lining can coordinate or contrast with the outer fabrics.

Tote Bag

You will need

- Two patchwork panels for bag sides (see step 1)

- Canvas or denim for bag base, top and handles:
  two pieces the same length as the blocks x 2½in (6.4cm) wide,
  one piece the same length as the blocks x 6½in (16.5cm) wide
  two 12½in x 4in (31.7cm x 10.2cm) strips for handles

- Sewing thread to tone with patchwork

- Quilting thread to tone with patchwork (if machine quilting)

- Plain calico (muslin) to back the side panels, larger than the patchwork panels

- Wadding (batting), larger than the patchwork panels

- One piece of fabric for bag lining the same size as the bag panel (see step 5)

Finished size: 18in x 14in (45.7cm x 35.6cm) approximately

Trusted Tip…

Adding a pretty lining to the bag tidies up the inside and can be a good place for a contrasting or colourful accent fabric. If you don't want to use patterned fabric, plain red or dark blue were once traditional kimono lining colours or try a bright patterned lining similar to *haori* (kimono coat) linings.

Cutting the Fabrics

1 Two patchwork blocks from the Masu Quilt were used to make this bag, but other blocks could be used. To make two blocks as in Fig 1, cut the following 2½in (6.4cm) wide strips for each block:
for outer 'box', two strips 14½in (36.8cm) and two 10½in (26.7cm),
for middle 'box', two strips 10½in (26.7cm) and two 6½in (16.5cm),
for inner 'box', two strips 6½in (16.5cm) and two squares each 2½in (6.4cm),
for the centre square, one 2½in (6.4cm) square.

Making the Blocks

2 Follow the instructions in step 3 for the Masu Quilt to make two blocks as shown in Fig 1. The blocks will be joined together later.

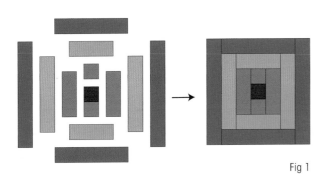

Fig 1

Quilting the Bag Panels

3 Layer and tack (baste) the bag ready for quilting, if quilting by hand or domestic machine – see Making a Quilt Sandwich. Quilt the patchwork pieces in the ditch around the seam lines. An extra quilting line can be added along the centre of each 'box' strip. Trim each panel and zigzag or overlock the edges before assembling the bag panel.

Making the Bag Handles

4 Using the two 12½in x 4in (31.7cm x 10.2cm) strips, make the bag handles as shown in Fig 2. Fold and press the strips, then machine sew close to the edges.

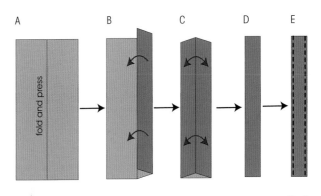

A   B   C   D   E

fold and press

Fig 2

Assembling the Bag

5 Using ¼in (6mm) seams machine sew the quilted blocks together with the bag base panel and top panels, as in Fig 3. Join the blocks with the 6½in (16.5cm) wide strip and sew the 2½in (6.4cm) wide strips at either end. Zigzag or overlock each seam. Press seams away from the patchwork blocks. Using the completed bag panel as a pattern, cut out a single piece of lining fabric the same size as the bag panel.

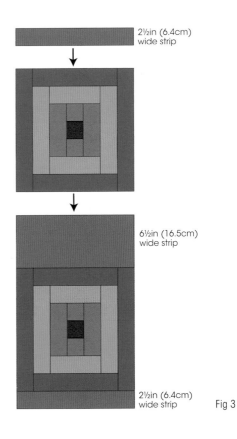

2½in (6.4cm) wide strip

6½in (16.5cm) wide strip

2½in (6.4cm) wide strip

Fig 3

6 Fold the bag panel in half right sides together so it looks like the finished bag. Machine sew the side seams using a ½in (1.3cm) seam allowance, starting and finishing each seam with a few backstitches. Fold and sew the lining fabric the same way, but leave a 4in (10.2cm) gap unsewn on one side, so the finished bag can be turned right side out through the gap. Press seams open.

7 Create the boxed base shape as follows. Keeping both bag and lining inside out, fold the bottom corners to make a point, as shown in Fig 4. Mark a line at right angles to the seam, 1in (2.5cm) from the point, then pin and machine sew across, creating a triangular flap of fabric. Cut off the flap, about ½in (1.3cm) from the stitched line, and discard the scraps.

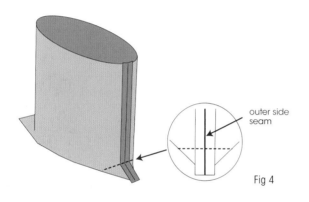

outer side seam

Fig 4

8 Arrange the handles on the right side of the bag panel as shown in Fig 5, allowing the handle ends to overlap the edge of the bag panel by ½in (1.3cm). The gap between the handle ends is 3½in (8.9cm) on each side. Make sure the handles are the same length and not twisted. Tack (baste) them in place.

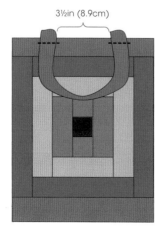

3½in (8.9cm)

Fig 5

9 Turn the outer bag section right side out. Keeping the bag lining turned inside out, place the bag outer inside the lining, lining up the top edge and the side seams. Machine sew around the top of the bag, sewing the lining to the bag outer all round with a ¼in (6mm) seam. Turn the bag right side out, through the unsewn gap in the lining side seam. Press the seam around the top of the bag. Machine or hand sew around the top of the bag, about ⅛in (3mm) from the edge. Turn the bag inside out, slipstitch the gap in the lining closed and then turn right way out and press to finish.

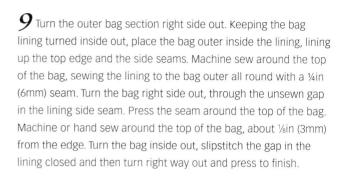

Trusted Tip...

Ready-made handles can also be used for a professional finishing touch. Leather handles are usually made for sewing straight on to the finished bag, while plastic or braided cord handles may be attached with fabric loops or wooden rings.

Equipment and Materials

The quilts and projects in this book require only the most basic cutting and sewing equipment – no specialist quilting rulers are needed and you don't need a sewing machine with dozens of fancy stitches.

Equipment

Rotary Cutter

Rotary cutting has made fabric cutting easier than ever, speeding up the task and enabling you to machine sew an exact ¼in (6mm) seam with the quarter-inch foot (using the cut fabric edge as a guide). Cutters come in various metric sizes – 28mm and 45mm blades are the most popular. Make sure the blade is clean and sharp as dull, nicked blades will skip threads and make cutting difficult (keep a spare blade handy). The safety guard is very important as the blade is *extremely* sharp, so always replace the guard after every cut. See Rotary Cutting.

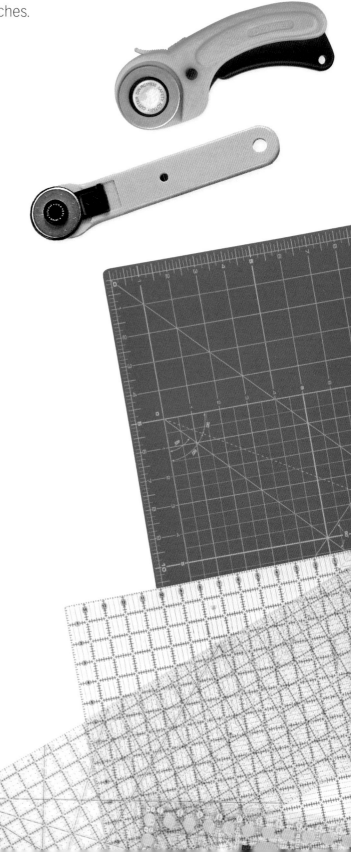

Cutting Mat

You must use a self-healing cutting mat with your rotary cutter, to protect your table and make sure your cutter blade stays sharp. Choose a mat marked with imperial or metric measurements, depending on which system you use. Most have imperial on one side and metric on the other. Use the measurements on the mat to help you cut larger pieces but check the mat and ruler measurements are the exactly the same first. Prolong your mat's life by cutting smaller pieces on different areas of the surface and cutting with the lines on the ruler whenever possible, rather than along the lines marked on the mat. Keep the mat away from heat and direct sunlight or it will warp.

Quilter's Ruler

This transparent, wider-than-normal ruler marked with a grid is an indispensable tool for rotary cutting and for marking quilting lines. Imperial quilter's rulers are divided into inches and fractions of an inch, to ⅛in (3mm), while metric quilting rulers are marked in centimetres, half centimetres and quarter centimetres. Many have 45 degree lines too, useful for cutting fabric on the bias (see Binding). Rulers 6½in (16.5cm) and 8½in (21.6cm) wide will be the most useful. Some rulers have a raised grid or gripper dots on the wrong side so it grips the fabric when you press down (you can add your own self-adhesive grips). Check measurements are the same between ruler and mat, or between rulers if more than one is used, as variations may occur.

Circle Templates

Use these to cut circles for the Kunimoto Quilt and Sakiori Quilt. You can make your own from cardboard or template plastic or buy a stacking set of acrylic circular templates in appropriate sizes for the quilt you are making.

Scissors

You will need a large pair of sewing scissors for cutting out curves and other similar tasks. Reserve your best quality scissors for fabric. Use your 'second-best' pair for cutting wadding (batting), as this can dull the blades. A small pair of embroidery scissors or thread snips makes trimming threads easy. Use paper-cutting scissors for cutting out freezer paper for appliqué.

Sewing Machines

You will need a reliable lockstitch sewing machine that can sew straight stitches. Zigzag or machine appliqué stitches are only needed for appliqué. There are a number of domestic machines made for quilters that are supplied with specialized presser feet (see picture below) and a range of stitches useful for quilting but most modern machines will be adequate. Use the correct foot for the stitch and test tension on scrap fabric before you begin. A walking foot is best for quilting straight lines and gentle curves – see Machine Quilting with a Walking Foot. You are unlikely to own your own long-arm quilting machine but many professional quilting services use these – see Using a Long-Arm Quilting Service.

Use an appropriate machine needle for your work and change it frequently – immediately if damaged or bent, if your machine starts skipping stitches or after several hours of stitching. A 'microtex' needle size 80/12 is good for patchwork in silk. A quilting needle is designed to stitch through several layers of fabric and wadding (batting) and so is ideal for machine quilting.

Other Useful Items

There are many items available to help with sewing but you really only need the following.

- ◆ You will need an iron and an ironing board for pressing patchwork. When pressing patchwork use a little steam and press carefully to avoid distortion. Use a steam iron and pressing cloth to press bag assembly seams after each stage of construction.
- ◆ A tape measure is useful for checking various measurements.
- ◆ 'Sharps' are the most useful hand sewing needles, for tacking (basting) pieces together and finishing off bias-bound edges.
- ◆ Fine, slightly flexible silk pins are good for pinning patchwork.

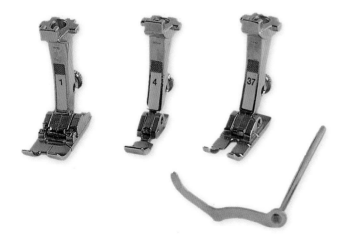

Presser feet (left to right):

Standard straight stitch/zigzag foot – for general sewing, utility and embroidery stitches. Use for machine quilting as the wide foot covers the feed dogs adequately.

Zipper foot – a narrower foot for sewing zips and piping.

Quarter-inch foot – essential for accurate patchwork. Can be bought separately and may vary slightly between manufacturers.

Quilting guide bar – for quilting parallel lines and grids. The guide slots into the back of the machine foot.

Materials

Threads for Patchwork

You will need good quality 50 or 60 weight cotton thread for sewing patchwork, with softer tacking (basting) threads for making the quilt 'sandwich'. Sludgy colours and greys are most useful. Polyester is stronger than cotton fibres and a polyester thread can eventually cut through fabric, so it is best to use cotton thread.

Threads for Quilting and Appliqué

Hand quilting threads are excellent for hand quilting but are not suitable for machine quilting. A 50 or 40 weight cotton thread is good for machine quilting or you could try a shaded thread. Use embroidery threads, such as perle cotton, coton è broder or sashiko thread for big stitch quilting by hand. For hand or machine quilting 'in the ditch' (along the seam line) choose a thread that blends with the fabrics so the quilting does not show. If you are using a professional quilting service ask the quilter to provide the thread.

Freezer Paper

Waxy freezer paper can be temporarily stuck to fabric by the heat of an iron and it is used as an iron-on template for the appliqués on the Kunimoto, Sakiori and Kimono Quilts and the Ranna Table Runner. It is most economical purchased on a roll but is also available in sheets. The white waxy wrappers from some reams of printer papers can be substituted.

Fabric Markers

Choose fabric markers that are easy to see and use and easy to remove after you have finished quilting. Tailor's chalk, quilter's marking pencils and Chaco liners (chalk wheels) are available in several colours.

Wadding and Backing

Quilt wadding (batting) is sold in standard sizes and by the yard or metre in various natural and manmade fibres. An 80% cotton 20% polyester blended wadding is suitable for hand or machine quilting. For a puffier, more three-dimensional effect a 100% polyester is good but is best hand quilted. For long-arm machine quilting ask your quilter for advice.

For backing, use good quality patchwork cotton, not sheeting. Backing and wadding should be about 3in (7.6cm) larger all round than the quilt top for hand quilting or machine quilting. For long-arm quilting, you will need to allow 6in (16.5cm) extra all round in order that the quilt can be mounted on the quilting frame. Join pieces with ½in (1.3cm) vertical seams, pressed open, or buy wider quilt backings. Avoid placing backing seams centrally or where a quilt will be folded.

Techniques

This section describes the basic techniques used in this book, including quilting and binding. The specific patchwork method used for each quilt is described in the relevant chapter.

Rotary Cutting

A standard ¼in (6mm) seam allowance all round is added to all patchwork pieces when cutting out. Sew this allowance accurately with the quarter-inch foot on your sewing machine for accurate patchwork without templates.

Cutting Fabric Strips

Square off uneven fabric ends before you start. Specific cutting instructions are included in each chapter. Turn the mat through 180 degrees and line up the parallel line on the ruler. Line up your rotary cutter against the ruler's edge and cut (see pictures A and B). Cut the larger pieces you need first, as the smaller pieces can be cut from the remainder of the fat quarter – the individual quilt instructions tell you when and what size to cut. You can cut strips very economically to standard sizes for squares and rectangles, such as 2½in (6.4cm) squares and 1½in x 2½in (3.8cm x 6.4cm) rectangles from the same 2½in (6.4cm) wide strip (C).

Cutting Safety

The rotary cutter has a *very* sharp blade and it is easy to cut yourself or others. Please follow these safety tips.

- Always cut away from yourself. Hold the cutter firmly in the same hand you write with, at a 45 degree angle. Hold the ruler in place with your other hand.
- Cut with the blade against the side of your ruler – on the right if right-handed and on the left if left-handed. The patchwork piece you are cutting is under the ruler.
- Use a sharp blade that is free from nicks and other damage. Using a dull blade requires more pressure when you cut and risks the blade slipping.
- Stand up to cut and place the mat on a firm surface – a kitchen counter or sturdy table is ideal.
- Always replace the safety guard on the cutter, and make a habit of doing this after every cut.
- Wear shoes in case you drop the cutter.
- Keep cutting equipment away from children and pets.

A

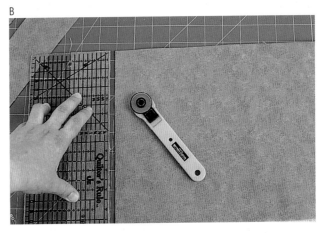

B

C

Machine Piecing Patchwork

Place your first two pieces right sides together, making sure the edges to be sewn line up. Set your sewing machine to a slightly shorter than average stitch length (about 1/16in/2mm) and check the tension is even. Use the quarter-inch foot and line up the fabric edge with the edge of the foot when you sew (see picture below). Some quarter-inch feet have a guide plate on the right-hand side so the fabric can't be sewn with a wider seam. Sew a slightly scant 1/4in (6mm) seam, as the pressed seam allowance and thread take up a tiny amount of the width too. Check your seam allowances by sewing some sample strips together, pressing all the seams to one side and measuring across – is the measurement as expected? If not, adjust your seam allowance.

Chain Piecing

Chain piecing whenever possible will speed up piecing patchwork. When you have sewn your first two pieces together, don't cut the thread. Place the next two pieces together and sew them a stitch or two after the first two pieces (see picture below). Continue like this to make a 'chain', which can be cut up afterwards. When chain piecing strips, pin them together in pairs and hold the end of the strips under slight tension as they are fed through the machine, so the ends match up neatly.

Trusted Tip...

If your machine tends to loop up the first few stitches, use a piece of scrap fabric as a 'leader' when you begin and chain piece the first two patchwork pieces on to that.

Pressing Patchwork

Press each stage of your patchwork as you go along, with the seam allowance to one side as this will help stop the wadding (batting) from 'bearding' or coming through the seam later. Pressing instructions are given in each quilt chapter. Press with a dry iron or just a little steam, using an up and down action so the patchwork is not stretched and distorted. Good pressing can really make a difference to your patchwork so get it right before you continue piecing.

Adding a Border

To sew on a straight border follow the instructions here or within the relevant project. If you want mitred borders you will need to add extra fabric for this. Sashing can be added in a similar way.

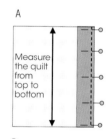

A

Measure the quilt from top to bottom

1 Measure the distance from top to bottom through the centre of your quilt top. Cut two side border strips to this measurement. Place the border strip right sides together with the quilt top, matching edges and pin in place. Use a 1/4in (6mm) seam to sew together. Repeat for the other border strip. Press seams towards the border or darker fabric.

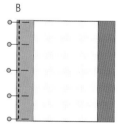

B

C

2 Now measure the quilt top from side to side across the centre. Cut two top and bottom border strips to this measurement and add to the quilt top as before.

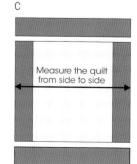

Measure the quilt from side to side

Sewing a Part-Sewn Seam

Part-sewn seams are used in some of the quilts to create a woven, unending look to borders or sashing. The diagrams below show the method used in the Irori Quilt.

1 Begin by stitching the first strip to the centre square but stopping after about 1½in (3.8cm) is stitched, as shown in Fig 2A and 2B and indicated by the blue line. Press the seam outwards.

2 Machine sew the next strip to the side of the block, as shown in Fig 2C. Continue adding strips in this way until the block is complete, then finish the first seam, overlapping the stitches by about ½in (1.3cm) (Figs 3D–F).

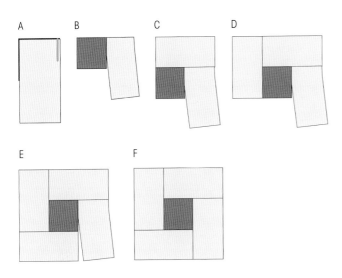

Appliqué

The easy appliqué used for the Kunimoto, Sakiori and Kimono quilts uses freezer paper ironed on the back of the fabric. A ¼in–⅜in (6mm–1cm) applique hem allowance is folded over the paper edge and pressed. The appliqué pieces can then be hand or machine stitched. Many machines have an appliqué stitch – two or three straight stitches followed by a very narrow single zigzag – and the machine hemming stitch can be shortened and narrowed to be almost identical. For hand appliqué, follow the diagram, stitching with the appliqué hem towards you and with stitches about 1⁄16in (2mm) apart.

The appliqué templates can also be used for bonded appliqué, using a fusible web product to iron on the appliqué following the manufacturer's instructions. Choose a bonding product designed for stitched edges, as it will be softer than one which basically fuses the appliqué without needing any stitching and leaves the fabric very stiff. Edge the appliqués with a small zigzag or machine blanket stitch. No appliqué hem allowance is required.

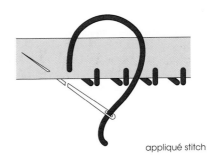

appliqué stitch

Making a Quilt Sandwich

The quilts and projects need layering with backing fabric and wadding (batting) – see Backing and Wadding before hand or machine quilting, except for long-arm machine quilting – see Using a Long-Arm Quilting Service. Press the patchwork and backing fabric. Place the backing right side down on a flat surface, using masking tape to hold larger panels in place. Lay the wadding on top and smooth it out. Place the patchwork on top, making sure there is wadding and backing behind all the patchwork. Use a quilter's ruler or measure across the quilt in both directions diagonally to check that the patchwork panel is square (i.e., right angled) and not distorted.

Pin or tack (baste) the three layers together. Pin with curved safety pins about 3in (7.6cm) apart, but take care when machine quilting near pins and remove them as you go. To tack, work from the centre outwards in a radiating pattern or across the quilt in both directions to make a grid, about 2in (5cm) apart. Once the quilt sandwich has been prepared, you are ready to quilt.

Quilting

Whether you quilt by hand or machine, the quilting stitches hold the patchwork, wadding (batting) and backing together, as well as adding a three-dimensional quality and sometimes extra patterns to the quilt. Free-motion machine quilting on a domestic machine is an art in itself and beyond the scope of this book, but you can free-motion your quilt tops if you wish.

Hand Quilting

Many quilters quilt using a hoop or frame, but I work without, tacking (basting) the quilt thoroughly instead. Aim for small, evenly spaced stitches. Start by tying a couple of knots in the thread about ½in (1.3cm) apart and 'pop' the knot through the top fabric, making a long stitch in the opposite direction to the way you will quilt and coming up at the start of the quilting line. Your first few stitches will catch the starting thread and secure it. With your non-stitching hand under the quilt, take several small running stitches at a time, going through all the layers, before pulling the thread through. At the end, turn the quilt over, tie two more small knots in the thread and pop these through the backing to finish off.

Sashiko-Style 'Big Stitch' Quilting

Thicker thread and larger stitches are used on several quilts in a style similar to traditional Japanese sashiko quilting, using light-coloured threads to show up the pattern. Stitch as for hand quilting, but make the stitches larger and use a larger needle with a long eye and a thicker thread – cotton perle No. 12, coton à broder and fine sashiko cotton are all suitable. For a more authentic sashiko look, make the gaps about half the length of the stitches.

Machine Quilting with a Walking Foot

A walking foot is necessary for smooth straight-line machine quilting. It synchronizes with the feed dogs to 'walk' all the layers of the quilt sandwich through at the same rate so the patchwork top doesn't pucker, distort or form ridges. To avoid wobbly quilting lines, change the throat plate to a straight stitch plate if possible, which will make your quilting stitch straighter. However, you *must* remember to change back to the zigzag plate before trying to stitch any sideways stitch patterns.

Machine quilting gives a distinct line which can be used to emphasize the patchwork by quilting 'in the ditch' or along the patchwork seam line, on the other side of the seam from the patchwork seam allowance, or to add another simple pattern on top of the patchwork. If your machine has the facility, set it to the 'needle down' position before you start quilting, so it will stop with the needle in the fabric. Some machines have a half-speed feature that slows the stitching down, which you may find useful.

With the machine feed dogs set 'up' and the walking foot attached, you can quilt in straight or gently curved lines. Working from the top, the walking foot helps to evenly feed all the layers through the machine at the same rate, working in unison with the feed dogs. Make sure the needle is down in the fabric before raising the presser foot to turn corners. Finish off the thread ends by hand sewing them into the quilt.

Using a Long-Arm Quilting Service

More and more quilters are having quilts professionally quilted on a long-arm machine. The quilt, wadding (batting) and backing are mounted on a frame and the machine moves along to quilt the design, either hand guided or computer controlled. The machine is able to quilt elaborate curved patterns that would be difficult to achieve on a domestic sewing machine.

The quilting may be split into hand-guided or free-hand patterns and pantographed or computer-controlled designs, with some quilters specializing in one style. Discuss your quilt with your quilter, who will help you select the best pattern and thread colours. Quilts with large pictorial elements, like the Furoshiki, Kimono and Hanui quilts, suit free-hand quilting, while repetitive designs like the Masu and Irori quilts look good with all-over repeat patterns. Check with your quilter before using silk in your quilt, as some quilters may prefer to work only with cotton.

The quilter will be able to advise you on wadding and threads and often supply these for you, as materials suitable for domestic machines may not work well on high speed long-arm machines. The quilt does not need to be tacked (basted) before being mounted on the frame. Deliver your quilt with the back as neat as possible, without loose threads which can get hooked up by the machine needle. Many quilters also offer a binding service. Allow plenty of time for the quilting and remember popular quilters may be booked up months in advance. All the quilters who worked on the quilts in this book are listed in Suppliers.

Tying

Instead of securing the layers of the quilt sandwich with quilting stitches, the layers can be tied together. Lay the quilt flat, right side up. Thread a needle with a long doubled length of embroidery or sashiko thread. Insert the needle from the front of the quilt, taking a backstitch through all layers of the quilt and leaving a 3in (7.6cm) tail of thread on the front. Tie off the thread securely with a square or reef knot and trim the thread ends to about 1in (2.5cm) long. Repeat the ties at regular intervals over the quilt sandwich, or where instructed in the quilt instructions.

Binding

The quilts in this book are bound with 2½in (6.4cm) wide strips, folded and pressed to make a doubled binding. Strips are cut either across the fabric, like the printed bindings on the Sakiori Quilt and the second Furoshiki Quilt, or on the bias, like most of the solid-coloured quilt bindings. Bias binding is more hardwearing. Join strips with seams at 45 degrees to the edge, as shown, and press in half lengthways. Mitred corners are easy to do.

1 Machine sew around the quilt, ⅛in (3mm) from the edge. Pin the doubled edge of the binding to the bottom edge of quilt, lining up with the quilt edge, as in diagram A. Leaving the first 10in (25.4cm) or so unstitched, machine sew the binding to the quilt, stitching one third of the folded width away from the quilt edge with a few backstitches. This ensures the binding will be a snug fit when folded over. Stop stitching with a few backstitches the same one third-width away from the end of the side.

2 Fold back the binding strip at 45 degrees and pin, forming the mitre, as shown in diagram B. Fold the binding strip back over to continue sewing to the side of the quilt and pin (C). Continue sewing the binding to the quilt and repeat this step at each corner.

3 Open out the start of the binding and cut on a 45 degree angle, re-fold and pin along the quilt edge. Pin the other end of binding along the last side of the quilt. Where the binding ends meet, trim

this other end on a 45 degree angle to match the slope at the start of the binding strip, adding a ½in (1.3cm) seam allowance to the end, as shown in D. Overlap the ends and sew together with a ¼in (6mm) seam. Press seam open. Finish sewing the binding along the side of the quilt.

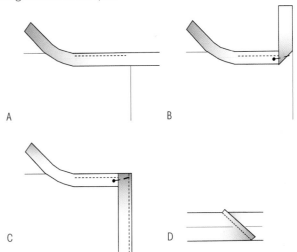

4 Turn the quilt over and using a hemming stitch (E), hem the folded edge of the binding to the back of the quilt, mitring corners neatly (F and G).

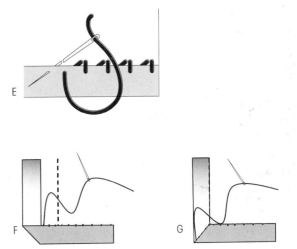

Quilt Labels

Add a simple label to your quilt when finished. If the backing fabric is pale or has light-coloured areas, you can write on to the back of the quilt using an acid-free permanent fabric marker. Alternatively, cut out a simple shape from plain fabric, press a ¼in (6mm) hem all round and hand appliqué to the back. Sign and date the label and include any other information you like.

Suppliers

United Kingdom

Susan Briscoe Designs
Yamadera, 4 Mount Zion, Brymbo,
Wrexham LL11 5NB
Email: susan@susanbriscoe.freeserve.co.uk
www.susanbriscoe.co.uk
*For vintage Japanese fabrics
(mail order only)*

The Cotton Patch
1285 Stratford Road, Hall Green,
Birmingham, West Midlands B28 9AJ
Tel: 0121 7022840
Email: mailorder@cottonpatch.net
www.cottonpatch.co.uk
*For fabrics and quilting supplies
(mail order and shop)*

Euro Japan Links Ltd
32 Nant Road, Childs Hill, London NW2 2AT
Tel: 020 8201 9324
Email: eurojapanlinks@aol.com
www.eurojapanlinks.co.uk
*For Japanese textiles, patchwork and
sashiko supplies (mail order only)*

Quiltessential
Arkwright's Mill, Mill Road, Cromford,
Derbyshire DE4 3RQ
Tel: 01629 825936
www.quiltessential.co.uk
*For fabrics and other quilting supplies
(mail order and shop)*

Step-by-Step Patchwork Centre
Barnstaple Road, South Molton,
Devon EX36 3RD
Tel: 01769 574071
Email: konaanne@aol.com
www.stepbystep-quilts.co.uk
*For fabrics and other quilting supplies
(mail order and shop)*

America

Debsews Fabrics
P. O. Box 161285, Honolulu, HI 96816
Tel: 808-221-5055
Email: debsews123@yahoo.com
www.debsews2.com
For Japanese fabrics (mail order)

eQuilter.com
5455 Spine Road, Suite E, Boulder CO 80301
Tel: USA Toll Free: 877-FABRIC-3
or: 303-527-0856
Email: service@equilter.com
www.equilter.com
For fabrics and quilting supplies (mail order)

Hancock's of Paducah
3841 Hinkleville, Paducah, KY 42001
Tel: Domestic US: 1-800-845-8723
Tel: International: 1-270-443-4410
www.hancocks-paducah.com
customerservice@hancocks-paducah.com
*For fabrics and quilting supplies (mail order
and shop)*

The Shibori Dragon
11124 Gravelly Lake Drive SW,
Lakewood, WA 98499
Tel: 253-582-7455
Email: shiboridragon@juno.com
www.shiboridragon.com
For Japanese fabrics (mail order and shop)

Australia

Be Be Bold
25 Elton Street, Lismore, NSW 2480
Tel: 61 2 6621 9188
Email: pjmacdon@bigpond.net.au
www.bebejapanese-textiles.com
*For Japanese fabrics (mail order and by
appointment only)*

Maleny Magic Patchwork and Quilts
924 Maleny-Montville Road, Balmoral Ridge,
QLD 4552
Tel: 61 7 5499 9954
Email: quilts7@bigpond.net.au
www.malenymagicpatchworks.com
*For fabrics and supplies (mail order
and shop)*

Fabric Panels

Alternative fabric panels can be used for the Furoshiki and Hanui quilts, but if you would like to use the same, or similar, panels to those in the book, the following information may be helpful.

- Cotton *furoshiki* like the rabbit and moon panel used for the Furoshiki Quilt are available by mail order from Gary Bloom in Kyoto. Email: bennettbloomers@gmail.com Gary also sells via Kyoto Kimono, based in the US (www.kyotokimono.com) – go to the 'Kyoto Collection' section. This rabbit and moon *furoshiki* is made in Kyoto by Marutaka, a member of *Kyoto Furoshiki*

Shin Kou Kai (the Furoshiki Study Group, the organization of traditional *furoshiki* manufacturers).

- The panel used for the second version of Furoshiki is from the 'Fuji Afternoon' range by Springs Creative – www.springscreative.com
- The koi panel and border used for Hanui Quilt is from the 'Kingyo' collection from Red Rooster Fabrics – www.redroosterfabrics.com

Long-arm Quilting Services

The following quilters contributed to this book and can stitch similar designs on your quilt.

Ferret

(Furoshiki and Kunimoto – free-hand quilting)
Ferret Fabrications, 11 Grosvenor Avenue, Harrow, Middlesex HA2 7AR, UK
Tel: (020) 88616410
Email: contact@ferfab.co.uk
www.ferfab.co.uk

Karen Florey

(Kimono – free-hand quilting)
The Running Chicken Quilting Co., Elizabeth House, 7 The Beeches, Tilehurst, Reading RG31 6RQ, UK
Tel: 0118 942 4085
Email: karen@therunningchicken.co.uk
www.therunningchicken.co.uk

Maria Laza

(Sensu and Shimacho – free-hand quilting)
Budapest Quilt Studio, Budapest, Tarkony u. 68.1028, Hungary
Tel: +3630 294 1523
Email: maria.laza@quiltstudio.eu
www.quiltstudio.eu

Leslie Carol Taylor

(Sakiori – computerized quilting)
North Sea Quilters, Van Bommellaan 36, 2245 VN, Wassenaar, Nederlands
Tel: +31 (0)6 2511 3010
Email: design@northseaquilters.com
www.northseaquilters.com

Linda Paris

(Igeta, Irori and Masu – computerized pantograph quilting)
Mobile: 07973 436656
Email: linda_paris@hotmail.com
www.linda-paris.co.uk

Acknowledgments

I would like to thank my family and my quilting friends, especially Annette Chadwick, Bet Coops and Deborah Gordon who helped with finishing the quilt bindings; Guy, Fluff and Takenoko; my friends in Yuza-machi and Yamagata Prefecture in Japan, who helped me discover so many of my inspirations for these quilts and whose friendship made my time in Japan so enjoyable; Bernina – my 153 Quilter's Edition sewing machine stitched everything beautifully; the owners of the very authentic Japanese Garden & Bonsai Nursery, in Newquay, Cornwall (www.thebonsainursery.com), where we photographed the quilts. Finally, many thanks to all the team at David & Charles for producing another gorgeous book.

About the Author

Susan Briscoe writes and designs for patchwork and quilting magazines and teaches patchwork and sashiko quilting in the UK and overseas. A graduate of UCW Aberystwyth, she began quilting after working as an Assistant English Teacher on the JET (Japan Exchange Teaching) programme in Yuza-machi, Yamagata Prefecture, Japan, in the early 1990s, where traditional textiles, architecture, landscape, the tea ceremony and local festivals provided inspiration. Specializing in Japanese textile themes, she has written over ten books on quilting, including three books on patchwork bags and two books on Japanese sashiko. Susan lives in North Wales, UK.

Index